Jonas Hanway

Domestic Happiness, Promoted

In a Series of Discourses from a Father to His Daughter on Occasion of Her Going

into Service

Jonas Hanway

Domestic Happiness, Promoted
In a Series of Discourses from a Father to His Daughter on Occasion of Her Going into Service

ISBN/EAN: 9783337817343

Printed in Europe, USA, Canada, Australia, Japan

Cover: Foto ©Thomas Meinert / pixelio.de

More available books at **www.hansebooks.com**

Domestic Happiness, promoted;

IN A SERIES OF

DISCOURSES

FROM A

FATHER TO HIS DAUGHTER,

ON OCCASION OF HER GOING INTO SERVICE;

Calculated to render SERVANTS in general

VIRTUOUS AND HAPPY:

WITH

VARIOUS CHARACTERS, ANECDOTES, FABLES, AND REFLECTIONS.

Being for the most Part adapted also to the

USE OF SUNDAY-SCHOOLS;

Abridged from VIRTUE IN HUMBLE LIFE,

WRITTEN BY JONAS HANWAY, ESQ.

A NEW EDITION WITH ALTERATIONS.

LONDON:

PRINTED FOR J. SEWELL, CORNHILL; AND
F. AND C. RIVINGTON, NO. 62, ST. PAUL'S CHURCH-YARD.

1795.

Description of the Frontispiece.

BEHOLD a *Father* worthy of the name,
His heart replete with ev'ry pious wish
And tenderness, which marks his character:
See him present his *Child* to *Industry*,
The fruitful source whence food and raiment rise
Under the *blessing eye of Providence!*
Erect in posture, and with solemn air,
Religion, with her sacred volume spread,
Invites her votary to read and mark:
With awful voice she speaks——
" Let not a single day unheeded pass
" Neglectful of the page, guiding thine heart
" To everlasting peace, and joy sublime!
" Behold, with wonder and with pure delight
" How gracious Heav'n, in mercy to thy wants,
" Most lib'rally bestows its various gifts:
" Contemplate then from whence these gifts proceed!"
The *Earth* displays her treasures and her charms,
While *dove-like* innocence attends the *scene!*
Near to yon sacred *venerable pile*,
Where many an honest villager has pray'd,

In steadfast hope of everlasting joy,
Stands a blest *mansion* deep embower'd with *oaks*,
(Our country's fortress and security)
Where peace and hospitality reside.
It is the seat of her whose virtues shine,
With all the splendor which adorns her sex.
Wishing to serve the fair industrious maid,
With all the care which Charity inspires.

   May gratitude and love combine, to give
Their souls an earnest of the bliss to come:
Then shall they live secure, securely die,
In joyful hopes of *everlasting peace!*

ADVER.

ADVERTISEMENT.

AN abridgement of "*Virtue in Humble Life*" was firſt made with the approbation of the pious and benevolent Author, for the uſe of a Charity School under the patronage of ſome ladies of fortune in the neighbourhood of *Pomfret* and *Leeds*; and it was afterwards enlarged by Mr. Hanway himſelf. As this little book has always been deſervedly held in high eſtimation for the excellent inſtruction it contains, and the ſpirit of piety and benevolence which marks every page of it; there cannot be any need of an apology for endeavouring to reſcue from oblivion a work which could not be loſt without injury to ſociety. The Editor of this new edition, therefore, produces it to the world, in full confidence of its meeting with a welcome reception from all who wiſh to promote piety and virtue among the claſs of people for whoſe uſe it was principally composed. When compared with the last edition, this abridgement will appear to have undergone some alterations; but they have been chiefly those of omission with a design of limiting the instruction to the lower orders in society.

INTRODUCTION.

Farmer trueman whose character is displayed in so exemplary a manner in the following pages, is supposed to have been one of the domestic servants of a single gentleman, who instead of indulging himself in the idle dissipations of fashionable life, employed many hours in studying how to benefit his fellow-subjects. As Thomas Trueman had not occasion to follow his master (as many footmen, unfortunately for them, are obliged to do) to play-houses and other places of amusement, he had a great deal of leisure time, which he wisely devoted to the improvement of his mind; and by reading and observation, he at length acquired sufficient knowledge to qualify him, when he afterwards became a parent, for the instruction of his own daughter in the most important concerns of human life. He esteemed this child, as a charge committed to his care, that he might train her in the paths of virtue and piety, in order to make her useful and comfortable in this world, and happy to all eternity in the next. He knew, that education and habit make *saints* or *sinners*, and prepare us for *both* worlds, or *neither* of them. As a christian, and a father therefore, he strove to inspire the heart of his child with just and exalted notions, such as are most graceful to human nature, and most acceptable to GOD.

Mary Trueman was worthy of all her father's care; in her infancy she was docile and obedient; and as she advanced in years she improved in every thing that is lovely in youth, and was particularly distinguished for neatness, gentleness, and modest deportment. As this amiable young creature had had the misfortune to lose her mother, her father was very solicitous to place her in service, under the care of some good lady, who would pay attention to her principles and morals, and give her occasionally, that counsel and admonition, which young people, however well-disposed, or carefully educated, frequently stand in need of. His enquiries

enquiries proved succefsful, and after having fully satisfied himself, that the lady was such an one as he could depend upon as the protectrefs and advifer of an innocent and artlefs young woman; that her family was governed with regularity; and that due regard was paid in it to religion, he sent Mary to wait upon her, and offer her services; the lady was so pleafed with Mary's appearance and manner, and had conceived so high an opinion of her from the account she had had of the pains her father had taken in her education, that she immediately hired her.

Before his daughter went to service, Farmer Trueman gave her the excellent advice contained in the following difcourfes, which we earneftly recommend to the ferious confideration of every parent and young perfon into whofe hands they may fall; as they point out in a ftriking manner, the duty, both of thofe who have children to fend forth into the world, and of thofe who in their early years are obliged to leave the paternal roof, and feek fubfiftence for them-

themselves. How happy would it be for society in general, if all parents in humble life, were like this worthy farmer, attentive to the *substantial good* of their children, instead of forming schemes for their *temporal advantages* only; and how many young women would be preserved from seduction and other evils, if the principles of virtue and religion were impressed upon their minds in their early years! Then we should not see domestic servants emulous to outvie each other in dress and appearance, eager to partake of pleasures and amusements unsuitable to their station, and scorning the authority of their employers; but on the contrary, we should view them, striving to excel in those qualities which alone can render them truly amiable and happy. Of all the tender relations in which we stand, none exceed that of a father towards his child, whether son or daughter; but the latter seems to be the most interesting to the heart, because the female is the least capable of defence: but if young persons receive no instruction either from books or conversation,

sation, is it to be expected that any great degree of virtue will exist in their hearts? Parents who are careless of their own souls cannot be supposed to be watchful over the souls of their children. Those who neglect to give their children the best advice in their power have much to answer for.

In every station of life the virtue of one sex depends greatly on the virtue of such of the other sex as they may chance to be connected with, particularly in their youthful days. The young female who is to make her way in a world full of snares and temptations, stands in particular need of good instruction. This abstract of "*Virtue in humble Life*" furnishes such admonition as appears to be necessary for them; and being expressed in persuasive terms, without any enthusiastic flights, and given in the tender character of a father, the instruction comes home to the bosom, it may therefore prove acceptable to such parents as are not qualified of themselves to teach their children the rules of piety and virtue by which they ought to regulate their conduct; and also, to young perfons who have no benefit from parental inftruction, but are able to *read* for their improvement—the latter may make good *Farmer Trueman* fupply the place of a *father* to them, by refolving to be guided by his excellent advice; and may extend the benefit to their youthful companions of either fex, by reading to them, what is fo admirably fuited to every *fon* and *daughter* in *Humble Life*.

CONTENTS OF DISCOURSES.

I. GENERAL exhortation to the duty of prayer. The goodness of God expressed in the works of creation — Page 1
II. The duty of keeping holy the sabbath day. Appeals by public worship on all great occasions - - 6
III. The great advantage of regulating the hours of prayer, as a guard against negligence - - 10
IV. Mistakes in relation to prayer. How they may be rectified. Advantages of a religious conversation. Family prayer. Respect for the clergy - - - 15
V. On the person of Christ. The extreme perverseness of the Jews in respect to him. And their present deplorable situation 21
VI. A manual consisting of exhortations, prayers and devotions for the use of my daughter Mary, aged 17 years, on occasion of her going into service: with extracts from archbishop Synge, on the Sacrament of our Lord's Supper, and reflections on the folly and danger of neglecting it, presented by her most affectionate father, Thomas Trueman, aged threescore and seven, 1777   25
viz. Morning hymn on waking, or - - ibid
    Morning ejaculation, on waking - , 26
    Ejaculation for night, in bed - - ibid
    Evening hymn - - - ibid

PRAYERS.

I. For the morning - - - ibid
II. Ditto by Bishop Kenn - - 27
III. For the evening - - ibid
IV. Ditto by Bishop Kenn - - ibid
V. For benefactors - - 28
VI. For humility - - ibid
VII. For obedience to parents - - 29
VIII. For fidelity in servitude - - ibid
IX. For patience, particularly in servitude - 30
X. For application to business, and resignation to providence ibid
XI. For chastity - - - 31
XII. For constancy of mind, and divine assistance ibid
XIII. Against censoriousness - - 32

XIV.

CONTENTS.

XIV. For grace to refist anger, pride, and unquietnefs Page 33
XV. Againft a foolifh, turbulent, impatient, or feditious fpirit - - - ibid
XVI. For a hufband, or a wife - - ibid
XVII. For children - - - 34
XVIII. For pardon of fins, in ficknefs - 35
XIX. For refignation in ficknefs - ibid
XX. For following the example of pious perfons - 36
XXI. For a good life and a happy death - ibid

HYMNS.

I. For gratitude - - 37
II. For protection from wicked perfons - 38
III. Againft flattery - - 39
IV. On the fhortnefs and vanity of life - ibid
V. For repentance and truft in God - 40
VI. The Chriftian's contemplation - ibid
VII. On the excellency of the Bible and Teftament 42
VIII. The Chriftian's hope - - 43

CELEBRATION of our LORD's SUPPER.

I. General preparation - - 44
II. Confeffion of fin - - 47
III. For divine affiftance - - 48
IV. On behaviour at the communion - ibid
V. After leaving the communion table - 49
VI. Prayer for refolution - - 50
VII. For charity - - ibid
VIII. Behaviour after the fervice - - 51
IX. Prayer for gratitude - - ibid
X. General rule in regard to the facrament - 52
XI. Reflections and expoftulation on the foregoing, and the danger of neglecting this memorial - - ibid

VII. Reflections on the archbifhop's fentiments and advice. The grofs folly of falfe reafoning in relation to our Lord's Supper, and the grofs ignorance frequently difcovered by thofe who neglect this effential part of their religion - 53
VIII. The miftrefs's efteem for fervants, agreeable to her fteady principle of religion and piety. Honefty in fervants with a prudent conduct. The difcretion of mafters and miftreffes effential to domeftic peace and happinefs. Character of an excellent female fervant. Humility neceffary in all ftations 64

IX. Danger of servants in changing places. The conduct of favourites towards fellow-servants. Behaviour of mistresses. Civility. Cleanliness. Caution against fire   Page 73

X. The advantages of temperance. Propriety in the dress of servants. Danger of crouded meetings. Effects of the undistinguished use of tea   -   -   79

XI. Character of the mistress. Her charity, punctuality, dislike of cards. Calmness of temper, religious chearfulness, &c.   82

XII. Reflections on the vicissitudes of human life. The sorrows it is subject to, and the liberality of nature in affording us comfort   -   -   -   86

XIII. Thoughts on the importance of time. Calculation of the probable duration of life. Thoughts on death   -   91

XIV. The indispensible condition of happiness in a life to come. Deaths of many persons of distinguished characters under particular circumstances of repentance   -   96

XV. The comparative characters of men and women, as displayed in their last hours. Deaths and behaviour of distinguished persons, particularly Amelia and Eleanor. Duty of comforting and exhorting our friends on their death-bed   -   105

XVI. Reflections on the certainty of death, and the resurrection. The New Testament our only guide. The character of our Saviour as described in it   -   -   117

XVII. On superstition. Folly of believing in witches. Story of Dame Tempest. On enthusiasm. On melancholy   125

XVIII. Charity for differences in opinion. The great importance of a good conscience   -   -   131

XIX. The advantages of humility. On a low station. A virtuous and vicious conduct contrasted. The fatal consequences of vice   -   -   -   137

XX. The great advantages of patience and caution in domestic service. Danger of censoriousness   -   142

XXI. The great importance of truth, and the infamy and punishment of lying   -   -   147

XXII. The detestable qualities of pride and vanity. Story of a miserable prostitute. On vanity, and the danger of flattery 152

XXIII. On envy, malice, revenge, cunning. Anecdote of a girl who lost her lover by discovering her propensity to envy   158

XXIV. The danger of an eager pursuit of pleasure. On amusement, choice of company, and conversation, as the safeguard of life   -   -   -   161

XXV. Generosity. Charity. Character of *Mrs. Ann Saracen*. Reflections on it. Ability to do good in the humblest fortune
   166

XXVI.

XXVI. Duty of learning to read. Reading the scriptures essential to religion. On writing. Frugality. Prudence. Fable of the wolf and the lamb. On modesty. Bashfulness   Page 172

XXVII. The advantages of friendship. Caution in respect to it. Necessity of circumspection in love   -   176

XXVIII. Warning against seducers to prostitution. Danger of going to London. Of being fond of fine clothes. Duty of chastity on christian principles. Danger of listening to superiors in fortune. Melancholy story of Caroline   184

XXIX. Advantages of the marriage state, when carefully engaged in. Fable of the two hounds. Dangerous effects of jealousy. Story of Harry Winter. Story of Jane Sprightly. The great duty of tenderness for children   -   191

XXX. Conclusion of advice recommending filial piety, obedience to parents, and fidelity in service   -   198

XXXI. Conclusion. Prayer for repentance and reconciliation adapted to the state of human nature, and such as believe in Christ   -   -   -   202

DISCOURSE I.

General exhortation to the duty of prayer. The goodness of God displayed in the works of creation.

WELL, MARY, thou hast seen the good lady: as she approves of thee, I hope thou wilt like to serve her. Sit down; I have *much* to say to thee, if my heart is not too full.

Thy dear mother is gone before me, and left me to act for her; and happy it is for thee that I am alive; for young women, particularly of thy condition in life, when deprived of their parents, are so much at their *own disposal*, that they often dispose of themselves very badly.

Methinks a separation, after seventeen years tender acquaintance with thee, even from thy birth, will be like parting with the blood that streams through my heart; especially as thou art going into a world with which thou art not acquainted. Believe me it is a bad world in many respects, but yet not quite bad, as some good people imagine. Whether it will prove to thee a good or a bad world greatly depends upon thyself: if thou wouldst have it a good one, turn aside from every evil way, and cleave to goodness.

..Remember thou hast a Heavenly Father, in whose sight I am but a miserable sinner. To his Providence I recommend thee. If thou art true to him, he will never forsake thee! *O God, preserve my child! keep her from presumptuous sins; cleanse her from those secret faults which cleave to our imperfect nature; and make her acceptable to thee, whom I have sought to serve, by breeding up my child in thy fear!*

Thou canst not easily conceive, MARY, how dear thou art to me: but while I employ my thoughts, and indulge my anxious wishes to preserve thee, I also consult my own happiness with regard to both worlds: so hath the wisdom of the Almighty ordained, that good intentions, and good actions, are ever self rewarded.

NEVER FORGET TO PRAY.

The first and greatest object of religion, next to the belief in a God, is to worship him. Now whether thou doest this in public or in private, take the wise man's advice: " Before thou prayest, prepare thyself, and be not as one that tempteth the Lord." Remember that there are two branches of devotion, *supplication* and *praise:* The *first* is the *confession of sin and misery,* and petition for relief; the *last* is an angelical and heavenly duty. The distinction is obvious; but I fear it is not made so often as it should be, and the reason is but too plain; people n general are not sufficiently attentive to their prayers; many utter words without praying.

My

My dear MARY, whether thou lookest up to heaven, or down upon the earth, if thy thoughts are not dissipated, like the thoughts of a child, thou wilt see infinite reason to adore thy maker.

There is no discouragement in the duty of *prayer:* There is no bodily labour in the discharge of it, unless it be spun out beyond measure. All rational exercises of religion are in themselves highly pleasant. *God* never *made* any reasonable creature *shy* of his company, and *averse* to his will. We see no inferior being disinclined towards its chief good, or negligent in pursuing its proper happiness; but this neglect of prayer demonstrates the corruption of our nature, and our departure from what man was *originally made.*

The gracious and awful presence of God, and the continuance of his blessing towards us, is not only necessary to our success, but also to our being. When I go into my fields, MARY, I look up with delight towards the heavens; but where the stupendous height of them ends, is past searching out: I can only *adore* and *wonder!* When I arise to my work, and behold the glorious appearance of the *sun,* I consider it as a " marvellous instrument of the work of the most high and eternal God." When I behold its effects shewn by day, I rejoice: when I consider it as the means whereby my blood circulates in my veins, and gives motion to my pulse and heart, I fall down in gratitude, not to the *sun,* but to *Him* that made it, and rules its power! The sun is also the instrument which animates even the clod of earth, making the grain shoot from its bosom, and in due time bringing it to maturity, for the use of man. Were the earth to be kept bound in the winter's frost, I need not tell thee that my labour in sowing would be lost.

How incomparable is the beauty of the heavens, and the clear firmament in fine weather! Is not thy heart enraptured when thou considerest whose handywork it is? Does not the spring and summer charm thee with the melody of birds, the verdure of the earth, and the refreshing stream? Canst thou see a rainbow and not praise him that made it? "Very beautiful it is in the brightness thereof: It compasseth the heavens about with a glorious circle, and the hand of the Most High hath bended it."—Hast thou considered how often the showers refresh the earth, when it is weary with drought, and as they fall bring with them marrow and fatness, to cheer the hearts of men and beasts? The snow also bringeth plenty on the earth, by the manure contained in it, or by the warmth of its covering. Hast thou never stood in religious reverence, though I hope with no childish fears or foolish dread, while thunder and storms made this globe of earth as it were to tremble? And when the lightning comes with astonishing swiftness, art thou not struck with awe? Canst thou forbear to say,—Great, O Lord, and wonderful are thy works?

As the day declares the power and glory of God, so also does the night. When thou retirest to refresh thy wearied limbs, MARY, consider every
star

star hung out as a lamp to shew thee God's marvellous power and wisdom!—Consider that God also made the moon "to serve in her season," as the months roll round, "for a declaration of time," and a sign that time itself will have an end.

All these wonders in the heavens remain in astonishing order, "and never faint in their watches."—They move at the commandment of the Most High, and without his all-wise direction, we mortals could not exist: We should be devoured by fire, or drowned in water, or chilled to death by cold. Thou, my child, wouldest fall like a leaf in autumn, even in the spring and blossom of thy life.

Accustom thyself to think that God is all in all, and let this thought influence thy practice. "When thou glorifiest the Lord, exalt him as much as thou canst, for he will ever far exceed thy utmost praise; put forth *all thy strength* therefore, *and be not weary.*" Our praise is grateful though it be weak. O my daughter, *God is all in all!* " He hath made all things, and to the godly he hath given wisdom."

Surely blind are those who will not see the glory of God displayed in his works! and deaf are those who will not hear the voice, either of reason or faith, though these proclaim their commission as received from heaven!

DISCOURSE II.

The duty of keeping holy the sabbath day. Appeals by public worship on all great occasions.

I CHARGE thee, my daughter, to pay a strict regard and reverence to the sabbath of the Lord. What would become of religion among men, if it were not for this holy day?

The neglect of this day has been the great inlet to all manner of wickedness. There needs no argument to prove that wherever the sabbath is broken, a whole tide of wickedness will flow in at the breach. And as God hath *blessed this day and hallowed it*, so they *unbless* themselves who profane it; and the keeping of it holy is one of the great duties of both Jew and Christian.

To the neglect or abuse of the sabbath we may impute many of the evils under which our country labours, in respect to sobriety and good discipline, reverence for laws, and such a regular uniform conduct as becomes good subjects and good christians.

Rejoice then, my dear, at the return of the sabbath, not so much that thou mayest then rest from thy labour, as I hope thou wilt be permitted to do, but that thou hast so fair an opportunity of offering up thine heart to thy maker. The Almighty has declared, that he is pleased with the worship of his rational creatures, when they assemble to make

joint

joint supplications for mercy for their offences. Go then with gladness to the house of God, not only to worship him, but to hear his word, from the mouth of his ministers. Those who have pleasure in praying to God, and who put their trust in him, instead of fleeing from church, repair to it, as the place of their highest comfort and joy: praise and thanksgiving is their delight, they pour out their hearts in humble acknowledgement of their sins past, renew their resolutions of amendment, and receive comfort.

The duty of attending divine worship is required of all christians, without distinction of persons. Those who seldom appear at church, are, generally speaking, either ignorant and abandoned wretches, who loiter about, seeking a miserable diversion of their thoughts; or poor children, who have nobody to instruct them.

As God has made a separation of the sabbath-day, for the purposes of religion by an absolute law; and as it is so happy a fence against impiety, it is amazing that it should ever enter into the heart of man to imagine, that God will dispense with the breach of it.

God requires obedience from us; and what is it which constitutes our chief glory but that very obedience? Where men are sincere towards God, they cannot be false to themselves or their fellow creatures: but what sincerity can there be towards their maker, if they decline the public worship of him, and as it were refuse to pay that public homage which is so infinitely due to the supreme Lord and proprietor of all? And behold, what is the consequence! How troubled and disordered, or how stupid and abandoned, does the mind of man become, when he ceases to rest his hopes on God! This is difficult to describe, but easily felt. If thou considerest the mercy thou receivest in the very breath thou drawest, thou wilt cry out with the Psalmist, " *Bless the Lord, O my soul, and forget not all his benefits. Who forgiveth all thine iniquities, and healeth all thy diseases. Who redeemeth thy life from destruction, and crowneth thee with loving kindness and tender mercies. Who feedeth thy mouth with good things, so that thy youth is renewed as the eagle.*" Thy devotion should indeed fly on the wings of love to the God that made thee.

It is the crime and misfortune of people in our condition, and perhaps of our *betters* also, that when we meet to worship God, we do not generally address him with that awe and homage which become rational creatures; and, as we justly stile ourselves, *miserable sinners*. My dear MARY, do always the best thou canst, and remember that however faulty some of our superiors may be, in their stations, the greater part of us are worse in ours, and therefore we should mend our own manners. There are many who know their duty, yet do not practise it; but when it happens that any superior does not shew us an example, it is in our power to put him to the blush.

What does the custom of our country, and our own reason, require upon all great events, in great
sick-

sicknesses, war or famine, heavy unseasonable rains or droughts; in all public distresses, or for public thanksgivings, but that we repair to the temple of God, there to pour out our hearts before him? If in him, and him only, we live, can we for a moment forget the vast obligation! Good God!—Is it possible to relate how negligent some are, as if they had not days enough in the week for loitering or for working! An idle person, at any time, is a bad sight; but absence from the great business of the sabbath-day, and during divine service, is monstrous indeed!

The false notions, joined to the rank hypocrisy of some of the Jews, in our Saviour's days, ran so high, that they pretended to be much scandalized at his doing works of mercy on the sabbath-day. This our Lord reprehended with severity, leaving us a lesson, that such employment ought not to be deemed as labour. Works of necessity are also warrantable, such as pulling the ox out of the pit. But what shall we say of those, who, having much time on their hands on this day, when the season will not permit them to walk abroad, employ themselves about any thing rather than in reading the scriptures, and pious and instructive books? How wretchedly do they murder their time!

Every thing good may be expected from persons who reverence the sabbath; but nothing worthy of praise can be hoped for, from those who withhold their homage to God on that day.

DISCOURSE III.

The great advantage of regulating the hours of prayer, as a guard against negligence.

OUR discourse yesterday, MARY, was very serious. Indeed it was in effect nothing less than a lesson of instruction to prepare for eternity: but I did not finish what I had to say.

What a deplorable condition are those in, who live all their days as *without God:* Can those who do not pray to him, MARY, be said to live *with* him?

The learned archbishop SHARP tells us, "*prayer* ought to be the continual exercise of life, for it is to our souls what meat and drink are to our bodies, their repast, their support, their nourishment. *Prayer* is the great universal instrument by which we fetch down blessings from above, and become possessed of whatever we want. *Prayer* is our defence and preservative against sin and against temptation. It is the wings of our souls, whereby we raise ourselves up above this lower world to the God above; with whom, while we therein converse, we become the more transformed into his nature. Whatever anticipations of heaven there be on earth, whatever foretastes we christians have in these bodies, of the happiness of eternity, they are all brought about by the means of prayer."

So

So says the pious prelate: and what christian, with any shadow of reason, ever attempted to contradict him? Yet there are such numbers who neglect their prayers, that thou wilt see many bad examples to one good one; and therefore thou must be guarded at all points.

Consider the necessity of being as active in thy religious, as in any other duties: this is a matter of the highest moment. The laziness which occasionally invades a great part of mankind, may happen sometimes to keep thee so long in thy bed, as to create hurry and dissipation of thought, by sudden calls to thy duty, which may prevent thy morning prayers; and thou wilt set about thy business without having offered up thy devotion. When this is the case, as soon as thou recollectest, repair the fault in the best manner thou canst. We may pray in thought, nay even in words, without acquainting the world what we are about. If after recollecting, thou declinest doing thy duty, and any evil should befal thee during the day, thou wilt suffer this double self reproach, that thou first omittedst thy duty, and then increasedst thy guilt by neglecting to ask for the protection of heaven: thou sufferedst business, or perchance some trifling object of amusement, to possess thy mind in preference to the God of thy salvation. And if no distinguished misfortune should happen to thee on that day, thou wilt be the more subject to the omission on another day, and accumulate thy guilt, and thy sins to be repented of. Nothing is more true in general, than that the omission

omission of good is in effect the commission of evil, and it is particularly true in this instance.

Be therefore sure of thy *morning prayer*; and rise *early*, that thou mayest not be interrupted in this duty. Habit will soon render it familiar, and thou wilt receive some part of thy reward in the benefits of early rising, which I need not tell thee, who art accustomed to enjoy this advantage.

There is the most respect, decency and propriety in praying on our knees. Prayers in bed are usually ejaculations or hymns; as when we are just falling into the death of sleep; or rising again, as it were from the grave, when we awake.

Make as sure of thy *evening prayer* also as of thy bodily *rest*, without which thou wouldst die.

My master once told me, that it is a proverb among the *Hollanders*, who are a busy nation, that " no one ever loses any time by praying, or is the poorer for giving alms." The first part is very obvious, and the last may be easily reconciled, where prudence is exercised.

Among various excuses for negligence, thou wilt hear some silly mortals plead *want of time*. This is as false in fact, as it is absurd in opinion; for if thou shouldst be interrupted in falling on thy knees in secret, pray as I have just mentioned, secretly as thou sittest, or walkest, or standest, or workest. But at all times when thou prayest, collect thy thoughts, that thy heart may keep pace with thy tongue. This is as essential a duty as it is to pray at all, and for the same reason short prayers are preferable

ferable to long ones. So far from pleading want of time, let not thy own heart admit of any excuse.

Our prayers are our true and faithful friends, which will never forsake us! We may enjoy the happiness and advantage of their company in a palace or a dungeon; and without their aid we cannot have the least security that we shall be constant to God, or live like believers in him, submitting to the laws of Christ. If thou dost not seek for the mercy of God, thou canst not expect to find it. Thou art commanded to seek, and promised *that thou shalt find if thou dost seek,* but not if thou seekest not.

Consider, my dear MARY, the state of human life, and the dangers which surround thee, and all the children of men. We are all subject, every day and every hour, to pain and sorrow, sickness and death; and should live prepared for whatever a day may bring forth. We are subject to a greater evil than the certainty of death; we are subject to *sin,* and therefore must take heed, whilst we think we stand, that we do not fall. Thou art sure that life must end in a few uncertain years. It is impossible, being in thy right mind, that thou should'st not be anxious for the event, what is to become of thee, that is of thy soul, through the numberless ages of eternity! We are all persuaded that we have souls, and believe they will be saved or damned. We are continually in hope or fear of something; and for the same reason that we believe in a state of rewards and punishments after death, our fears and hopes extend to objects beyond the grave.

Every

Every one knows this who is not stupid: what then canst thou do to take out the sting of thy fears, and to render thy hopes, not only comfortable but joyful? What canst thou do, but apply thine heart and understanding, all thy mind and all thy strength, to God? Consider, my child, how thou mayest most gracefully, and most willingly resign thyself to whatever shall please divine providence; always hoping for the best, so long as thou doest thy duty, and prayest to the great parent of mankind.

And what is religion, of which prayer is one of the highest acts, but the knowledge of the most excellent truths, the contemplation of the most glorious objects, the hope of the most ravishing pleasures, and the practice of such duties as are most conducive to our happiness?

Be well assured, MARY, and I think thou hast tried the experiment, thy inclination to serve God faithfully in thy thoughts, words and actions, will encrease with thy daily practice in the duty of prayer. On the other hand, if thou should'st forsake the paths of virtue, thou wilt as certainly forsake thy prayers, and thy inclination to goodness will daily decrease: of this I have known numberless sad and deplorable instances. Prayer prevents sin, as sin prevents prayer. To think of the mercy and goodness of God, and of trusting in him, is of the nature of prayer. But thou knowest that our Saviour requires of us to use words, but not vain speaking; therefore let thy words be few, because to be rendered valuable, they must be uttered in spirit and in truth. Heaven preserve thee, my dear daughter!

DIS-

DISCOURSE IV.

Mistakes in relation to prayer. How they may be rectified. Advantages of a religious conversation. Family prayer. Respect for the clergy.

MANY of us are apt to fall into a fault which seems to proceed from a right principle, though not rightly understood. Reserve is in no instance more proper than with regard to prayer; yet it is equally true, that a false reserve oftentimes betrays the cause of devotion. When people are afraid, or ashamed, of doing what is right, they are in the more danger of being led to do wrong. There is a kind of resolution so essentially necessary to religion, that it can hardly exist without it; not only with respect to the general habit of life, but as we are firm in supporting the cause of virtue, considering it as an unchangeable obligation incumbent on all the children of men. Women, in the first ages of christianity, opposed themselves to flames and tortures in the cause of truth, with as constant and intrepid a mind as the bravest man that ever lived. There is nothing great without constancy: and it is our duty to possess our souls with such resolution, that as no fear of pain should frighten, no temptation to pleasure should entice us from our duty. It is this habit of resolution which gives a lustre to all our actions, and over-balances or conquers

quers all the gilded charms of pomp, or the allurements of vice.

We are commanded, it is true, by our great Lord and Master, to pray in secret, that we may not be seen of men; that is, not to *seek* the eyes of men, as the Pharisees did. Thou rememberest our Saviour expressly mentions the gross hypocrisy of those people in his time. However do not turn away from the meaning of thy divine teacher, and act as if thou wert ashamed of being found on thy knees. The consequence of childish fear in this instance is, that many get into an habitual neglect, and do not pray at all. If two persons meet together, both well inclined, and both timorous, or prejudiced to this opinion, they will both decline doing their duty; and what a ridiculous, and at the same time tragical figure, will they make! If we come to the point of never praying but at church, can it be expected we shall be really attentive to our prayers when we are there? And can we pray at church without being seen? Custom makes it familiar to us to avoid all human eyes in private, and it is right to seek a retreat; but resolution, and attention to the great business of devotion, should render us superior to all interruption or surprise when we are praying.

Thy poor mother, with all her piety was some time before she surmounted that false modesty in which she had been bred, which made it seem criminal in her eyes to be seen on her knees; but thank God I happily convinced her, that as a mutual security

not

not to neglect the duty of prayer, according as we retired to rest and rose at the same hour, so we should jointly or separately offer up the incense of our prayers with one heart and one soul.

Thou art sensible, that in order to fix any object on the mind, we must think, or read, or discourse about it. The two last include the first; but there is a peculiar charm in the conversation of sensible pious friends; we are sure of their heart. My master used to say, that according to a Persian proverb, "*the conversation of a friend brightens the eyes.*" The familiar discourse of a virtuous friend is pleasing and advantageous; but of all conversation, that is the most interesting which has affinity with religion, and leads us into the path of righteousness. Such as this can hardly come from any but the good and wise: those only deserve the name of friends, who are true to their own hearts, and confess the power of religion; persons of a different turn can only do us kindnesses, and be agreeable companions. If thou would'st be wise, thou must sometimes submit to be thought foolish. The first thing a wise man considers, is *the end of his being*; the next, how he shall attain that end; and thou mayest be well assured, whatever tends to promote the cause of true religion, goes so far in the attainment of the true end of life, and exalts human nature. Some of the truly zealous, and some of the enthusiastic part of us, talk of religion occasionally; but for want of distinguishing true zeal from enthusiasm, which is as different as light from darkness, many people

people are apt to draw a conclusion, that those who speak of piety are not pious in the sense that piety is allowed to be amiable, good, and praise-worthy.

In thy tender years, when thou didst pray, thou lookedst up to heaven, seeming to feel the force of thy words, and to mean what thou saidst. Cherish this custom, and hold it nearest to thy bosom. Thou hast sometimes seen thy mother on her knees, with streaming eyes, entreating the Almighty to pity thy poverty and thy sex, and shield thy person from the merciless hands of the vile destroyers of female innocence. Thou art now arrived at years of discretion, and knowest thine own danger; therefore thou must consider thine own prayers as thy surest guard: and if thou prayest to thy heavenly Father with real devotion, let the world go as it may, he who heareth in secret will reward thee openly.

HELPS IN PRAYER.

Among the various helps of performing the duty of prayer, I reckon it one of the greatest to utter words slowly and solemnly, weighing their sense and meaning. Whether it be the comfort or advantage, the pleasure or glory of praying, it must arise from a close attention to the object to whom thou dost address thy prayers. Thy attention must be kept awake, that thou neither tire nor wander in thought. These infirmities are indeed much alike, and human nature is much addicted to them. A book at church is of great use to some; it prevents the eye from wandering; the more thou perceivest thyself addicted to this weakness, the more watchful thou must be

of

of thyself, and accommodate thy prayers to thy real powers of mind; at the same time do not deceive thyself, and under a fond notion of an unavoidable defect, become habitually negligent. Our hearts are more treacherous than we are apt to imagine. It is certain that a multitude of words will not avail; but if thou art indolent, cold, and unwilling to pray, thou mayest perchance think a *few* words are too many. In such circumstances thou canst not be said to offer up thy heart to God, be thy words few or many.

A consciousness of the weakness of our nature, respecting our inability to expand the wings of our devotion, beyond a certain measure, may so far turn to our advantage, that it should naturally create a humiliation of heart, which is one of the essential requisites of piety, and constitutes a chief part of it.

FAMILY PRAYER.

Family prayer is another means to help us in the duty of devotion. This is a mutual security to all persons in the family, that they shall say their prayers at certain times, whether it be once or twice in a day. If such prayer be properly repeated, they will rouze the powers of the mind, and conquer that coldness and unwillingness which is apt to seize the heart in this instance, if we do not keep a strict watch over it. But family prayer is so much out of fashion, thou wilt rarely find it.

I fear that servants receive but little benefit from their master or mistress in this instance.

Thou

Thou seest then that this great business will depend generally on thyself.

In the comparative view of *private* and *public* prayer, thou oughtest to consider, that although it is the custom of the world to follow *example* rather than instruction, it is the safest way in most cases to follow the *instruction*——It is an indispensible duty to worship God in public; those who go to church chiefly from custom and decency, are seldom much inclined to devotion, public or private: and as to distinctions the same authority which requires public worship, requires private also. " The prayer of the *humble* pierceth the clouds, and till he come nigh he will not be comforted." This is not said particularly of *public* or *private* devotion, for it is supposed of the *humble*, that the same warmth and sincerity accompanies both. To *pierce the clouds* with our prayers, is a strong and beautiful expression; and it must be the importunity of our supplications, when they come from the heart, which can be supposed to reach the ears of the Almighty, or afford comfort or joy to the mind of man. Amidst all the bustle of the world, *I consider that person as the happiest of the children of men, whose addresses to God are the most acceptable.*

RESPECT FOR THE CLERGY.

If thou *fearest God*, thou wilt respect his *immediate servants*, the preachers of the gospel. The wise man considers it as a trial whether we love God or not, our *reverencing* or *forsaking* his ministers. And indeed it was natural for a wise man to draw

draw this conclusion, because in common life, in proportion as we love the master, we shew a proper regard to his servants. My dear MARY, consider it as thy indispensible duty to shew respect to this *order of men*, as immediately employed in the service of the great Lord of heaven and earth.

As a *father*, I *command* thee; as a *friend*, I *entreat* thee, to pray constantly and uniformly every morning and evening. Be assured, my daughter, that it is the means which will bring thee a blessing and success in life; and without it thou mayest easily stab my peace, and bring my grey hairs with sorrow to the grave. If thou pursuest my maxims, and obeyest my precepts, though we should be visited by the hand of adversity, yet our *lives* may be *comfortable*; and our *deaths*, when heaven shall call us hence, will open to us a passage to a joyful and glorious eternity!

DISCOURSE V.

On the person of Christ. The extreme perverseness of the Jews in respect to him. And their present deplorable situation.

CONSIDER, my dear MARY, the dignity and character of the person whose intercession and mediation with God, and for the sake of whose merits, thou hopest for the mercy thou askest for in prayer—even the Prince of Peace! When he made his

his triumphant entry into *Jerusalem*; (not with the splendid shew of an earthly monarch, to please the fancies of men, with a tinsel glitter, but to fill the heart with joy, even to the hopes of heaven and happiness immortal,) the multitude that followed shouted " *Hosannah to the Son of David. Blessed is he that cometh in the name of the Lord!*"—Blessed indeed was he who had power to open the eyes of the blind, to enable the dumb to sing, and the lame to dance for joy! Yet such was the fatal blindness and perverse disposition of the rulers of the *Jews*, that they *condemned* this glorious prince of Peace, this Sovereign of the universe, to die upon the cross. And what heart can conceive, or what tongue can utter the dreadful scene, then represented on the theatre of the world! Thou rememberest, MARY, what thou hast read in the New Testament, concerning the sufferings of our blessed Redeemer—when he bowed his head and gave up the ghost; the earth trembled; the veil of the temple was rent; the rocks burst; many of the dead arose, and appeared before men's eyes; all nature seemed for a time to be convulsed, and, as it were, expiring with the Son of God!

Such was this great event, and thus did the Almighty ordain from the beginning, that his *Son should die* to redeem a sinful world, and to rise again from the dead the third day in triumph over the grave. But what was the consequence of this *unparalleled* obstinacy and wickedness of the *Jews*, who were the voluntary instruments of this act of

cruelty

cruelty and injustice? their famous city of *Jerusalem*, with their holy temple, was, forty years after, destroyed by the *Romans*. *Jerusalem* is now in the hands of *Turks*, and of very little account, though once the pride of the whole earth. And as to the *Jews* themselves, their state was destroyed, and the people dispersed over the earth; and now for near seventeen hundred years the Almighty hath not permitted them to collect themselves into a body, or form a government, but they have been scattered in *christian*, *mahometan* and *pagan* countries; manifesting to the whole earth the truths of the gospel of Christ. Thou beholdest some of their descendants, who live among us: to this day they maintain their particular customs and manners; they neither keep the *same sabbath day* that we do, nor eat the flesh of animals killed after the same manner. They do not mix with the world as soldiers, seamen, or husbandmen; they intermarry only among themselves: in a word, they stand as *monuments* to remind us of the crucifixion of Christ, though themselves are *unbelievers*, and still look for that very *Messiah* whom their forefathers crucified, as we declare in our *belief*.

There are some of our condition in life, MARY, so little instructed in relation to prayer, that they do not distinguish the *Belief*, or declaration of what they believe, from an address or prayer to the Almighty. There is indeed this likeness, that both are of a serious and solemn nature, and require a close attention to the sense of every word, that sufficient time be given for recollection, and assent of mind, to the full meaning of them. Serious attention is the *first* step towards religion: The *second* is the knowledge of the *commandments of God:* The next is a firm and steady resolution of *obedience* to such commandments; and *lastly* our *prayers,* imploring the divine assistance: these mutually aid and support each other, and employ their joint forces in combat in sin, and triumphing over the world.

If thou believest the resurrection of the body, and the life everlasting, and that Christ will come to judge the living and the dead; remember that at the last day thou thyself wilt be among the number of one or the other of them—Christ will certainly judge *thee.* If thou shalt have earnestly endeavoured to live according to thy belief, and agreeably to the commandments of God, and the precepts of the gospel, thou wilt be happy for ever!—really, truly, and substantially happy in the endless ages of eternity! If thou hast not so lived, but shalt be found in a state of impenitence, thou wilt perish everlastingly!

A MANUAL

CONSISTING OF

Exhortations, Prayers, and Devotions,

FOR THE USE OF

MY DAUGHTER MARY;

AGED SEVENTEEN YEARS;

on occasion of her going

INTO SERVICE:

With Extracts from Archbishop SYNGE on the Sacrament of our Lord's Supper, and reflections on the folly and danger of neglecting it,

PRESENTED

By her most affectionate Father

THOMAS TRUEMAN,

AGED THREE SCORE AND SEVEN,

1777.

Morning hymn.

"LORD, hear the voice of my complaint,
    Assist my secret prayer;
To thee alone, my King, my God,
    Will I for help repair.

Thou in the morn my voice wilt hear,
    And, with the dawning day,
To thee devoutly I'l look up,
    To thee devoutly pray."

Morning ejaculation, on waking.

Unto thee I lift up mine eyes, O thou that dwelleſt in the heavens. Early in the morning do I cry unto thee! Incline my heart, O Lord, that I may call my ways to remembrance, and diligently obey thy commandments, through Jeſus Chriſt my Saviour. Amen.

Ejaculation for night, in bed.

Keep me, O Lord, by thy Almighty power, and preſerve me from the dangers of this night. Blot out my tranſgreſſions, and when my laſt hour ſhall come, let me paſs from life to death: and receive me, O God, into thy eternal reſt, for Jeſus Chriſt his ſake! Amen.

Evening hymn.

O may my ſoul in thee repoſe,
  To thee, great Lord, her fears reſign;
And grant my eyes in peace may cloſe,
  Confiding in thy pow'r divine.

Then when the ſleep of death ſhall come,
  With *faith* and *hope* let me obey
Thy will, which calls me to the tomb,
  Expectant of eternal day!

PRAYERS.

1. *For the morning.*

MOST merciful God, the mighty guardian and protector of mankind, who haſt ſafely brought me to the beginning of this day, I beſeech thee to continue thy mercies to me! Ponder my words,

words, O Lord, and confider my meditation! I am going into a world furrounded by fnares, and befet with temptations: let the remembrance of thy goodnefs, and the repeated mercies which thou haft fhewn to me, keep my gratitude in all its vigour; and let the hopes of thy future favour add ftrength to my vigilance and care. Guard my heart, and keep the door of my lips, that I may never trefpafs on thy righteous laws! This I beg, O merciful God, for the fake of my bleffed Redeemer. Amen.

2. *For the fame, for a young perfon, by Bifhop Kenn.*

O MERCIFUL God, keep, and protect, and blefs me this day, profper me in my calling; and preferve me from fin and danger, through Jefus Chrift my Saviour. Amen.

3. *For the evening.*

O GOD, the fure defender of all who put their truft in thee, I moft humbly befeech thee to keep me this night under thy protection: let thy Almighty power fhield me againft all dangers; defend me againft all affaults of my fpiritual or bodily enemies, and make me to dwell in a fafe and peaceful habitation. Grant this, O Father, through the merits and interceffion of thy Son, Jefus Chrift, the mighty Saviour of mankind. Amen.

4. *For the fame, for a young perfon, by Bifhop Kenn.*

I BESEECH thee, O merciful God, grant me true repentance, and thy holy fpirit, that I may live a godly, righteous, and fober life, for the fake of Jefus Chrift thy beloved Son. Amen.

5. *For benefactors.*

MOST merciful Lord, *the fountain of all good*, I beseech thee to extend thy favour and loving kindness to my friends and benefactors; reward them for the good which through thy providence they convey to me. Guard them from all *sadness* and *affliction* but such as may be instrumental to thy glory, and their *eternal welfare*. Preserve their persons from all *violence*; and let not the powers of darkness prevail against them. Guide them in thy paths, and make them the instruments of thy mercies to mankind; that amidst all the taunts and ingratitude of the world, they may stand as monuments of thy parental tenderness and care, and finally be received into thine everlasting kingdom, through Jesus Christ, the mighty Friend and Saviour of the world! Amen.

6. *For humility.*

MOST gracious and merciful God, who in thy great goodness didst send thine only Son upon the earth, grant that the example of his meekness and humility, his incomparable sweetness and condescension, may make the deepest impressions on my heart! Mortify in me all proud thoughts, and a vain opinion of myself, that I may neither boast of any thing which thou hast permitted me to possess, nor be unmindful of the hand from whence it came. Make me to know my own infirmities, that I may never seek my own praise, nor delight in that which may be offered to me by others. Let me glory in discharging my duty to thee, and in shewing due honour and respect to my fellow creatures, that at length I may receive the crown which thou hast prepared for thy faithful servants, in thy kingdom of eternal glory, through Jesus Christ, my blessed Lord and Redeemer. Amen.

7. *For obedience to parents.*

O ALMIGHTY Lord, and heavenly Father, who delightest in the obedience of children, I beseech thee give me a meek and humble spirit. Inspire my heart with an utter abhorrence of the dreadful guilt of undutifulness and disobedience. Let no falsehood or evasion betray my soul, but grant that I may dare to confess the truth, to those who have a right to require it. Make me patient under reproof, and diligent in performing my duty. Let my love, gratitude and submission to my parents, be accepted as obedience to thee, my Father and my God! Grant this, I beseech thee, O Lord, for Jesus Christ his sake. Amen.

8. *For fidelity in servitude.*

GREAT God, thou righteous judge of men! let thy fear be always before mine eyes, that I may discharge my duty with faithfulness and zeal. Let my conduct towards my superiors * express my gratitude for all the mercies which thou hast vouchsafed unto me. Thy all-piercing eye can see my inmost thoughts, and minutest actions! Let my fidelity and respect towards my superiors be apparent in their † sight, that I may delight in promoting their prosperity: and I beseech thee, to give

---

* Master or Mistress, or both.   † His, her, or their.

them such a just sense of their eternal obligations to justice and piety, temperance, and all other virtues, that *their* conduct may not disturb the repose of *my* mind, but uniting our endeavours in the advancement of thy glory, and the good of mankind, promote the happiness of every one. This I beg, O most merciful Father, through the merits of Jesus Christ my Redeemer. Amen.

9. *For patience, particularly in servitude.*

MOST merciful God, and tender Father, I beseech thee in thine infinite goodness to remove from me all pride and haughtiness of spirit, and teach me how to support myself under every circumstance of life; that with patience, resolution, and singleness of heart, I may subdue evil with good, and ever possess my soul in tranquility. Grant me grace to imitate the humility of my blessed Lord and Saviour, that I may obtain such peace of mind, and rest of soul, as the world cannot give. Let my conscience be always void of offence towards thee, and my fellow-creatures; that amidst all the follies and iniquities which surround me, I may acquit myself with applause in thy sight, O God, and receive the great reward which thou hast promised to thy faithful servants, through Jesus Christ my Redeemer. Amen.

10. *For application to business and resignation to providence.*

ALMIGHTY Lord, who hast ordained by thy unchangeable decrees, that man shall eat his bread in sweat and labour; give me, I beseech thee, an
active

active and industrious disposition. Let my diligence and innocency go hand in hand, and administer to their mutual support; that my life may pass in safety, and my death be full of hope. Teach me, O God, an entire submission to thy will! Give me so true a relish of my condition, that the glorious example of humility which Christ hath set before my eyes, may appear as far beyond any earthly advantages, as the glories of eternity outshine the transient splendors of this world. Thus resigned, O Lord, let me labour with my hands, in stedfast hopes of future happiness, through his merits who redeemed this sinful world. Amen.

11. *For chastity.*

MOST holy and eternal Father, I beseech thee let thy spirit descend upon thy servant, that my body may be undefiled from all impurities. Let no unchaste words pollute the tongue which thou hast commanded to be an organ of thy praise. Seal up my senses from all vain objects, that they may be fortified against the assaults of the prince of darkness; and by watchfulness and mortification, possessing my soul in true holiness, I may at length resign myself to death, in stedfast hope in thy mercy, to receive the reward which thou hast promised to thy faithful servants, in a joyful resurrection, through Jesus Christ my Redeemer. Amen.

12. *For constancy of mind, and divine assistance.*

HEAR me, O merciful Father, I humbly beseech thee, and let thy grace be ever present with thy weak unworthy servant. Regulate my affections and desires, and confine them to such objects as are pleasing in thy sight. I am not able of myself to do or think any thing that is good; O let thy spirit assist my poor endeavours. Vanquish the temptations which beset me! Fix my inconstant mind; and follow me through all my paths. Thou, Lord, art my hope!—thou art my rest!—in thee alone is pleasure and true satisfaction; and all without thee is misery and torment. O grant me the happy security of thy peace, that I may abandon all the false appearances of happiness here below, and find calm ease and sweet repose in thy love and favour. Hear my prayer, O merciful Lord of heaven! O hear me and have mercy on me, for the sake of Jesus Christ my Redeemer. Amen.

13. *Against censoriousness.*

O TENDER Father of mankind, correct in me, I beseech thee, whatever is malevolent or censorious; refrain my tongue from evil, and my lips that they speak no guile; that imitating the conduct of my blessed Saviour, by unfeigned love and true commiseration, I may mourn over the offences of others; and by my best endeavours make them sensible of the errors of their ways. If it be thy pleasure, let me suffer injuries, but not do them. Teach me, O God, to enter into the recesses of my own heart, and take an impartial view of my own sins; that avoiding all severe judgments of others, I may finally escape condemnation at the judgment seat of Christ, in whose most holy name I implore thy mercy! Amen.

14. *Fa*

14. *For grace to resist anger, pride, and unquietness.*

MOST righteous and just God, to whose all-piercing eye ungodliness and wrong are open as the day; grant, I beseech thee, that whatever injuries or provocations I may meet with in the world, I may discern the folly and wickedness of pride and anger, and meekly commit my cause unto thee, trusting in thine infinite wisdom and goodness for relief, through Jesus Christ my Redeemer. Amen.

15. *Against a foolish, turbulent, impatient, or seditious spirit.*

ALMIGHTY Lord and sovereign ruler of the world, give me I beseech thee, a due sense of obedience to my governors and superiors: that considering the weakness and infirmities of my nature, I may judge truly of offences. Guard me, O God, against that defection and rebellious spirit, which are the offspring of pride and ignorance; that the repeated dreadful punishment of thine ancient and peculiar people, and of the various nations of the earth, recorded for our admonitions, may inspire my breast with such sentiments as becomes my character as a christian. Grant, O Lord, that under this glorious calling I may contribute to the solid security of my fellow-subjects, and by my faithfulness in thy service enjoy the only perfect liberty. This I beg for his sake who died for his country and mankind! Amen.

16. *For a husband or a wife.*

MOST gracious Father, and eternal God, who hast consecrated the holy state of marriage, I beseech thee let not the cares and inquietudes, the weak-

weaknesses and infirmities, which cleave to our imperfect nature, discompose my spirit. Give me, under all the accidents and vicissitudes of life, a chearful and obliging temper, a strict attention to to my duty towards thee, with truth, fidelity and affection to my husband (or wife). Give me, O Lord, thy grace, that I may be a guide and good example to my family: that discharging all their respective duties in quietness, contentment and humility, thy blessings, O God, may rest upon them, and particularly on the person of my husband (or wife): and grant, O Father, that we may both live in mutual love, to the end of a holy and happy life, and finally be received into thy joys, for the merits of Jesus Christ our blessed Lord and Redeemer. Amen.

17. *For children.*

O GOD and Father of my life, whose goodness extends to all the children of men, I beseech thee let thy heavenly benediction rest upon those whom I devote to thy service, that they may act as the instruments of thy providence in doing good. Give them so just a sense of their duty, that by kindness and gentleness of manners, sobriety and zeal, and the fear of thee, O God, they may find the way to everlasting peace! Thou, who art the tender parent of mankind, O lead them by thy merciful guidance into the paths of righteousness; that *brotherly love* and *christian meekness* may be the law of *their* lives, and they the comfort and support of mine. Incline their hearts to piety, and their hands

to

to labour, that they may eat the bread of innocence. This I beg, O Lord of mercy, for the sake of Jesus Christ thy Son, who died upon the cross to redeem the world from *sin* and *folly!*

18. *For pardon of sins, in sickness.*

Hear me, O almighty and most merciful Father, and extend thy goodness to thy servant. Sanctify, I beseech thee, all thy corrections to me, that the sense of my weakness, in my present condition, may add strength to my faith, and seriousness to my repentance. Give me grace so to take this visitation, that if my sickness shall end my present life, I may be removed to those regions were sickness, pain and sorrow shall be no more, even to dwell with thee in bliss eternal, through the merits of my blessed Redeemer Jesus Christ. Amen.

19. *For resignation in sickness.*

Most righteous God, in whose hands are the appointments of life and death, grant that I may perceive thy justice and mercy, and look up to thee for strength to bear, and grace to profit by my sickness. Let me consider it as a scourge for my sins, and a medicine to heal the diseases of my soul. Grant, O Lord, it may answer these ends; that trusting in thy gracious promises, I may behave myself submissively, patiently, and devoutly; and if it be thy pleasure to restore me to health, let me constantly send up my heart in praise and gratitude to thee, and lead the residue of my days in thy service, and to thy glory. But if it be thy will that I now should die, O God forgive my manifold transgressions;

gressions; and prepare my heart, that I may stand accepted before thy throne. Receive me into thy favour, O Father eternal, for the sake of Jesus Christ, who died for the sins of men, and rose again for their redemption. Amen.

20. *For following the example of pious persons.*

O Almighty Father and God of Israel, who hast remembered thy most faithful servants with a peculiar mercy, leaving their example to all succeeding ages; grant that I may meditate on the conduct of such pious persons, as were most distinguished in their time, that devoting my heart to thee, I may never depart from thy truth and righteous ways. I praise thy holy name for all thy servants departed this life, in thy faith and fear, beseeching thee to give me grace to follow their *good example*, that with them I may be a partaker of thy heavenly kingdom. Grant this, O Father, for *Jesus Christ* his sake, our only Advocate and Mediator!

21. *For a good life and a happy death.*

O Lord and Father of my life, I behold my days passing away like a shadow: shed thy influence on my heart, that I may improve the remainder of them, and recover the precious time which I have lost! Instruct me, O God of wisdom, how to prepare myself for that hour, when I shall appear before thy judgment-seat! that being full of the hopes of a blissful immortality, I may rather desire than dread my dissolution. Thy eternal decree is past: it is appointed to man once to die: O teach me to meet the king of terrors without dismay: teach me to

receive

receive him as a welcome messenger, and whether early or late, let me joyfully obey thy summons! This I beg, for Jesus Christ his sake. Amen.

HYMNS.

1. *For gratitude.*

" WHEN all thy mercies, O my God,
  My rising soul surveys,
Transported with the view, I am lost
  In wonder, love, and praise.

O how shall words with equal warmth
  The gratitude declare,
That glows within my ravish'd heart,
  But thou canst read it there.

Thy providence my life sustain'd,
  And all my wants redrest,
When in the silent womb I lay,
  And hung upon the breast.

To all my weak complaints and cries,
  Thy mercy lent an ear,
Ere yet my feeble thoughts had learnt,
  To form themselves in pray'r.

Unnumber'd comforts on my soul,
  Thy tender care bestow'd,
Before my infant heart conceiv'd
  From whence those comforts flow'd.

When

When in the flipp'ry paths of youth
  With heedless step I run,
Thine arm unseen convey'd me safe,
  And led me up to man:

Thro' hidden dangers, toils, and deaths,
  It gently clear'd my way,
And thro' the pleasing paths of vice
  More to be fear'd than they.

When worn by sickness, oft hast thou
  With health renew'd my face;
And when in sins and sorrows sunk,
  Renew'd my soul with grace.

Through every period of my life,
  Thy goodness I'll pursue;
And after death in distant worlds,
  The glorious theme renew.

When nature fails, and day and night,
  Divide thy works no more;
My ever grateful heart, O Lord,
  Thy mercy shall adore."

  2. *For protection from wicked persons.*

"To God I cried, with anguish stung,
  Nor form'd a fruitless pray'r;
O save me from the lying tongue,
  And lips that would insnare.

Safe shall I go, and safe return
  While He my life defends,
Whose eyes my ev'ry step discern
  Whose mercy never ends!"

3. *Against flattery.*

"To Thee I call; O haste thee near;
  My voice, great God, indulgent hear;
With grateful odor to the skies
As incense let my pray'r arise,
And let my hands, uplifted high,
With full acceptance meet thine eye.
Let virtue's friends, severely kind,
With welcome chastisement my mind
Correct; but give not these to shed
The balm of *flattery* o'er my head,
Lest sudden from thy wrath, I feel
The stroke, that none can ever heal."

4. *On the shortness and vanity of life.*

"Hear, Lord, my pray'r, and let my cries
  Accepted to thy throne arise:
O turn not thou thy face away,
Nor longer my relief delay;
But mark my sorrow from on high,
And pitying to my call reply.
Fast as the mountain smoke decays,
On Time's light pinion flit my days:
As fades the shadow of the sun
With quick decline my moments run,
Just verging to their close: my face
Its vernal bloom and youthful grace,

Extin-

Extinguish'd withers on the eye,
As plants beneath a hostile sky.
But thou blest guard of Israel's fold
Shalt ages see, on ages roll'd,
And thron'd above, to endless days,
Extend thy honour, name, and praise."

5. *For repentance and trust in God.*

"LORD! to my wants thy ear incline;
  Behold me, as with grief I pine;
My hope confirm, and guard from ill
A soul subjected to thy will.
From rising to declining day,
To thee with fervent lips I pray:
Propitious to thy servant's heart
Thy chearing influence impart:
To thee, to thee I vent my care;
I know thee Lord, nor slow to spare,
Nor weak to vindicate from harm,
The soul with pure devotion warm.
My days with sorrow clouded o'er,
Thy wonted succours I implore.
Long as I breathe the vital air,
Thy love, my loudest praise shall share,
Whose aid my soul with health has crown'd,
And snatch'd me from the pit profound."

6. *The Christian's contemplation.*

"IN vain the dusky night retires,
  And sullen shadows fly:
In vain the morn with purple light,
  Adorns the eastern sky.

In vain, the gaudy rifing sun,
    The wide horizon gilds;
Comes glitt'ring o'er the silver streams,
    And chears the dewy fields.

In vain dispensing vernal sweets,
    The morning breezes play;
In vain the birds with chearful songs,
Salute the new-born day.

In vain, unless my Saviour's face
    These gloomy clouds controul,
And dissipate the sullen shades,
    That press my drooping soul.

Oh! visit then thy servant, Lord,
    With favour from on high,
Arise my bright immortal sun,
    And all these shades will die.

O when shall I behold thy face,
    All radiant and serene,
Without those envious dusky clouds,
That make a veil between?

When shall that long expected day
    Of sacred vision be,
When my impatient soul shall make
    A near approach to thee?"

7. *On the excellency of the bible and testament.*

"Great God, with wonder and with praise
    On all thy Works I look;
But still thy wisdom, pow'r, and grace
    Shine brightest in thy Book.

The stars, that in their courses roll,
    Have much instruction giv'n;
But thy good Word informs my soul
    How I may climb to heav'n.

The fields provide me food, and show
    The goodness of the Lord;
But fruits of life and glory grow
    In thy most holy Word.

Hear are my choicest treasures hid,
    Here my best comfort lies,
Here my desires are satisfy'd,
    And hence my hopes arise.

Lord make me understand thy law,
    Shew what my faults have been,
And from thy gospel let me draw,
    Pardon for all my sin.

Here do I learn how Christ has dy'd,
    To save my soul from hell,
Not all the books on earth beside,
    Such heavenly wonders tell.

Then let me search thy scriptures more,
    And with renew'd delight,
By day read all thy wonders o'er,
    And meditate by night."

8. *The christian's hope.*

"When rising from the bed of death,
    O'erwhelm'd with guilt and fear,
I see my maker, face to face,
    O how shall I appear.

If yet while pardon may be found,
    And mercy may be sought,
My heart with inward horror shrinks,
    And trembles at the thought.

When thou, O Lord, shall stand disclos'd,
    In majesty severe,
And sit in judgment on my soul,
    O how shall I appear!

But thou hast told the troubled mind,
    Who does her sins lament,
The timely tribute of her tears
    Shall endless woe prevent.

Then see the sorrow of my heart,
    E're yet it be too late;
And hear my Saviour's dying groans,
    To give these sorrows weight.

For never shall my soul despair,
  Her pardon to procure,
Who knows thy only Son has dy'd,
  To make her pardon sure."

"*Instructions for the proper celebration of our Lord's Supper*, by ARCHBISHOP SYNGE.

1. *Of general preparation.*

IF you would maintain and keep yourself in a constant *general preparation* for the holy communion, so as always to be fit, upon the shortest notice, to partake of it, (which every christian ought to endeavour after) be careful in the observation of these following rules.

1. Be diligent in your endeavours to know and understand the several parts of your duty to *God*, to *man*, and to *yourself*; for which end, you must be careful to make the best use you can of those means of instruction and knowledge which God has put into your power; such as reading the holy scriptures, and other good books, or hearing them read; attending upon the public offices of preaching, catechizing, and the like *.

2. You must, upon all occasions, be industrious and zealous in avoiding every sin, and in performing every duty according to your ability and opportunity †.

---

* Prov. iv. 5.   John v. 39.   2 Tim. iii. 15.   John xiii. 17.
† Tit. ii. 11—14.   Matt. vii. 21.   Luke xii. 47.

3. You

3. You must very often think and meditate upon your ways, and all your particular practices, and examine whether or no they are agreeable to the rules of your duty; that whatever you find you have been deficient in, or done amiss, you may take the better care to rectify and amend for the time to come *.

For which end and purpose, this following easy, but very profitable task, is recommended: namely, two or three times in the course of each day, to carry your thoughts back, and consider what you have been thinking, or doing, and how you have spent your time. As for example; ask yourself,

When first I awaked, did I think upon God, and recommend myself to his almighty care and protection? Did not worldly, or sinful thoughts, first take possession of my heart?

I was lately in such and such company; how and after what manner did I behave myself; were all my words and actions innocent, modest, and decent? Did I give no offence to God, or scandal to the world, by any thing which I either said or did on that occasion? &c.

Such questions as these, if you would constantly and seriously put home to your conscience, while things remain fresh in your memory, would have great influence upon you, to restrain you from evil, and excite you to do that which is good with joy and pleasure.

* Psalm iv. 4—and cxix. 59. Lam. iii. 40.

2. *Of particular preparation.*

I. Whenever notice is given of the celebration of the holy communion, immediately resolve by no means to miss that opportunity of commemorating the sufferings of your blessed Lord and Saviour.

II. In the midst of all your business, often call to mind, that such a day you must not be absent from God's holy table, and therefore be very careful not to do any thing which may render you unfit for it.

III. At some seasons it is very necessary that every man should set a little time apart for the more strict and particular examination of his conscience. But where a man often receives the holy communion, and never misses any opportunity for it, I do not conceive that such a particular examination is every time absolutely necessary; nor have all men, at all times, leisure enough for it: but no man ought to receive the holy communion without some previous examination of himself. For the more easy and regular performance of this, I would have you remember, that the whole duty of a christian is reducible to three heads*, and every time you receive the holy communion, you ought by all means to put at least these three questions seriously home to your conscience.

1. Do I effectually shew my love to God, by a due honour and respect to him in all my thoughts, words, and actions?

2. Have I a true and sincere love for myself: that is, do I love my soul better than my body? and

---

* Matt. xxii. 37, &c.

am I more heartily concerned to secure my everlasting happiness in the world to come, than to compass my pleasure or profit in this life?

3. Have I a real and sincere love for all mankind, without exception?—And do I avoid hurting any person by word or deed? (where I can possibly avoid it?)—And am I ready to do good to every one whatsoever, wherever I have ability and opportunity?

If you meditate on these three questions seriously for a little time, there is scarce any sin that you have been guilty of, but it will occur to you.

4. When by the examination of your conscience you have set your sins in your view, use in your ordinary devotions this, or some such like confession of them to God.

PRAYER.

2. *A confession of sin.*

"O MOST gracious God! I thy unworthy creature, humbly acknowledge my sins before thee. Besides those which I have now recollected, I lie under the guilt of many more transgressions, which I am not able to recount or remember. I have committed many sins, contrary to the motions of thy grace, and the light and conviction of my own conscience; and therefore do most justly deserve the severity of thy wrath and indignation against me. But, Lord, I fly unto thee for mercy! For the sake of Christ Jesus, my Redeemer, be merciful to me in the pardon of all my sins; and so guide and assist me by thy good grace, that for the time to come I

may

may be careful to abstain from every evil thing, and keep a conscience void of offence towards thee and towards mankind: This I beg, through the same Jesus Christ, my blessed Lord and Saviour. Amen."

3. *For divine assistance.*

"Most merciful God, who hast given thine only Son Jesus Christ to die for our sins, grant me thy grace, I humbly beseech thee, that I may never be unmindful, but always truly thankful for that inestimable benefit vouchsafed unto me by his death and sufferings; and so fit and prepare me, O Lord, by the assistance of thy Holy Spirit, that both at this, and all other times, I may be rightly qualified to commemorate the passion of my blessed Redeemer in that holy ordinance which he hath appointed; and also thereby effectually to partake of that redemption which he has wrought for all mankind. This I beg, through the same Jesus Christ our Lord. Amen.

4. *On behaviour at the holy communion.*

1. At the holy communion, as at all other times in the worship of God, strive as much as you can, to keep your mind intent and fixed upon what you are about; and lay aside not only all wicked thoughts, but likewise all such as are impertinent to the present business.

2. Take care to behave yourself with such outward decency and composedness, as may be a sufficient token of that inward devotion and reverence which you bear in your heart, without gazing about, or any way unnecessarily moving your body, or whis-

whispering to any one that is near you, or doing any thing of the like nature.

3. While the service is performing, join all along with the minister and congregation, with your heart and thoughts lifted up to God; and with your tongue also, where the liturgy requires that any thing should be spoken aloud by the people; as in the responses, the confession, the Lord's prayer, &c.

4. Take care, likewise, to avoid all affectation, and not to behave yourself in such a manner, as if you had a mind to be taken notice of for a person of extraordinary devotion. For which reason, whatever private prayers or meditations you may have to offer to God, put them up in your thoughts alone, let not your voice be heard, but when the public office requires it.

5. When you have received the Bread, offer up this, or some such short ejaculation to God:

O God! grant that by the suffering of my dear Saviour, who was crucified for me, I may escape eternal sufferings, and be made partaker of everlasting glory!

And when you have received the Cup, say thus in your heart:

O gracious God! grant that by the shedding of the blood of thy dear Son, I may obtain the remission of all my sins; and assist me, O God, to remember him with gratitude, praise, and adoration.

5. *After leaving the communion table:*

While the bread and wine are distributing to the rest of the congregation, entertain yourself with such meditations and prayers as these.

D   1. Bethink

1. Bethink yourself what those sins are, to which you have been most inclined; and in the presence of God, seriously and stedfastly renew your resolutions of being careful to abstain from them for the time to come.

2. Consider what opportunities you ordinarily have for the doing of any good works, and stedfastly purpose to be diligent hereafter in making use of them.

6. To this add the following prayer.

For resolution.

"Merciful God, assist me with thy grace and holy spirit that I may always keep those vows and good resolutions, which thou hast enabled me to make; that I may never return to any of my former sins, but hereafter serve thee faithfully in the constant practice of virtue and religion, through Jesus Christ our Lord. Amen."

4. And here express your charity, by putting up a prayer for all mankind in this or the like form:

For charity.

"Lord, if it be thy gracious will, extend thy mercy and compassion unto all mankind. Enlighten the minds of those that are ignorant, and move the wills of those that are obstinate, that they all may receive thy holy truth, and carefully live in the practice of it. Pardon my enemies, O Lord, and bring them, and all of us through the whole world, to true repentance, that we may all live righteously here, and in the end, be happy with thee hereafter, through Jesus Christ our Lord. Amen."

5. Then

5. Then entertain yourself with reading and meditating upon some select portions of the holy scripture, until such time as the minister is ready to proceed with the public office. I need not here transcribe any particular texts, but will leave you to make choice of such as are most agreeable to you. If you should be at a loss, read *the hundred and nineteenth psalm*, where you will easily find proper matter enough to employ your devoutest thoughts upon this occasion.

Duty after the service.

6. When the service is ended, and the congregation dismissed, depart to your home or place of abode, and as soon as you have a convenient opportunity of retiring into some private place, first look back, and consider whether or no, in the performance of this holy office, you have behaved yourself in all things as you ought to have done; and if you find that you have been any way short, or defective therein, resolve to take better care for the time to come.

7. And then conclude with this or the like prayer.

9. *For gratitude.*

"Lord, I desire to return my most humble and hearty thanks to thee, for all thy blessings, both spiritual and temporal, which thou hast vouchsafed to me. At this time particularly I praise and bless thy holy name, for the opportunity which thou hast this day given me of commemorating the death and passion of my blessed Redeemer, and of testifying my faith in the all-sufficient sacrifice which he made for the sins of mankind, by my participation of that holy ordinance which he appointed. Lord, pardon all my defects in the performance of this great duty. And I beseech thee assist me hereafter with thy grace, that in the whole course of my life I may ever be careful to fulfil and perform those vows and resolutions which I have made to thee, through Jesus Christ our Lord. Amen.

10. *General rule in regard to the Sacrament.*

Endeavour, as the occasion arises, to call to mind what you have thought, and said, and done, before and after the holy communion. And beg God to assist you, that you may remember your Saviour with constant gratitude, praise and adoration, that this remembrance may constantly restrain you from all manner of wickedness.

Upon the assault of any temptation thus bethink yourself:

"At such a time I received the holy communion, and then I seriously resolved, and solemnly promised to Almighty God, that I would heartily endeavour, in all points, to live like a *christian*. Shall I then, on any account, lye, curse, swear, talk profanely or obscenely, commit any sin of uncleanness, steal, cheat, or do or think any manner of wickedness? No: God forbid! I have engaged myself to God to mend my life, and to be another sort of person. And what can I expect but wrath and indignation from him, if *knowingly* and *wilfully* I should violate those promises which I so deliberately and steadfastly made to him."

DIS-

DISCOURSE VII.

Reflections on the Archbishop's sentiments and advice. The gross folly of false reasoning in relation to our Lord's Supper, and the ignorance frequently discovered by those who neglect this essential part of their religion.

SO far thou seest the sentiments of a very good and great man in the person of an Archbishop. Thou perceivest that he lays his stress on offences which ought to create an alarm, being *knowingly* and *wilfully* committed; not on infirmities and accidental trespasses. And what is the nature of wilful transgressions? Whether thou receivest or receivest not, these are high offences? What is thy baptismal vow? What is any thing relating to thy belief in the oracles of God, contained in the holy scriptures? Are not such offences forbidden? If thou neglectest the means of restraint which our Lord and Saviour has so mercifully appointed as a memorial of his death, and the reason for which he was pleased to suffer so much torture; with what degree of common sense canst thou, or any christian pretend, that it is better upon the whole to *neglect* those means than to use them? Will not the same reasoning hold for neglecting sober conversation, prayer, truth and justice, and a habit of every thing that is good and worthy of praise? All must arise from a sense of religion.

Believe me, my dear child, there never was an instance in any country, professing a belief of any kind, where a greater absurdity has been committed by creatures bearing the noble distinction of reason, than our neglect in this instance.

The principle of self-preservation is the strongest in nature, even in the brute which perishes. Shall man, the image of his maker, endowed with such noble faculties, the heir of the glories of immortality, vilify himself so much as to depart from his true interest and eternal happiness?

Christ is the great Captain of our Salvation. He commands us to *remember him*, and to do it in a certain manner. He does not leave it to us; but he says *Do this in remembrance of me*. It partakes of the greatest folly to pretend to be a sincere follower of Christ, and not to remember him in the manner he hath commanded. Thou seest by the little tract left us by an Archbishop, what he thought of this matter.

Let thy heart weep, my child, when thou hearest what I am going to say. I have great reason to fear there are many who live and die without receiving the sacrament of our Lord's Supper. Some begin late in life, and some neglect this duty, and leave off very early, either stupidly, or as they forget themselves and take to evil courses.

Negligence in this article arises from wicked or foolish reasons, or no reasons at all. People stand in awe of this solemnity, as of a very good and sacred institution, but do not partake of it, because they

they do not think themselves good enough; and they act as if they were determined to be no *better:* while they say with their lips it is very good, they act as if it were no means of making them good; which is a contradiction. They consider not that it is required by *Christ himself.*

We differ much in practice from the papists, who think themselves in a dangerous state without it: they ascribe to it marvellous powers, as if the priest had a faculty of converting bread and wine into the body and blood of Christ, which is contrary to our senses: but still they are sincere in their reverence of it.

I put it to this simple issue. If I were to invite my neighbour to sup with me, and he excused himself because his person was not in a cleanly condition, would'st not thou be astonished that he did not set about to wash himself? But supposing I were to furnish him with the requisites for making himself clean, and he still insisted that he could not come; shouldest thou not suspect that he was disinclined to my friendship, and sought for a reason to excuse himself?

It is a melancholy consideration, that we of this nation pretending to be so wise, should be so *foolish.* There is no miracle in the effects of this celebration: it neither saves nor destroys, but as it operates on the hearts, the lives, and manners of men like other religious duties; but this is of the greatest moment.

Our Lord and Master, the great Redeemer, in whom we profess to trust, invites us to his supper; as upon another occasion he says, "come unto me all ye who travel and are heavy laden, and I will refresh you." And can any one go to the supper of our Lord, properly prepared, and not feel himself refreshed in spirit? He directs us, on this occasion, the most solemn the world ever knew, to come to his supper. He, the Son of God, the Lord of Life, was going to die for us, and commanded us to do this in remembrance of him; and dost thou think, while memory holds a place in thy brain, thou oughtest *forget* him? He tells us *why* we should commemorate his death, and *how* it is to be done. He bids us receive the bread and wine in remembrance of his death and passion, of his body pierced, and blood spilt, as a token of his wonderful love towards us; and requires this memorial to be continued through every generation, until his coming again in glory, to judge both the living and the dead!

Good God! is it possible people can be such fools as not to see the force of this command? Would any person in his right mind, refuse such an invitation from the greatest and best friend in the world, upon so vast and important an occasion? Can any one decline coming to this heavenly entertainment, without a neglect which is an affront to so great a Lord of so great a feast?

If we consider the command, as coming from the great Captain of our salvation, is not our refusal to obey

obey it, of the same nature as a soldier's offence, when he disobeys his commander?

To reason calmly—we may ask in what consists the difference between a law which commands a thing to be done, and the same authority which orders a thing not to be done? "*Do this in remembrance of me*" is as absolute a command, as one of the ten commandments "*Thou shalt not steal.*" If thou dost steal thou knowest it is a breach of this commandment. If thou dost not receive the sacrament, and in this act remember *Christ*, is it not likewise an absolute breach of one of the laws of Christ?

I beg thou wilt observe that the intention of this celebration, ought to be considered in these several views.

1. It is to *fix* and *imprint* on our minds, in a manner the most *lasting*, the remembrance of the death of Christ, as the strongest motive to our obedience.

2. It is a commemoration of his death, in an humble acknowledgment of its being the *only ground of our hope of pardon*.

3. It is a public declaration to the world of our *faith* in him, and that we on our part, will endeavour to continue down the *memory of his love to all generations*.

4. It is the highest expression of our thanks and gratitude to God for his unspeakable mercy in sending his Son into the world for the redemption of mankind.

5. It is also a confirmation, on our part, of the covenant which God hath made with us, and a thankful acceptance of those *conditions of pardon*, which he has offered, and whereby we acknowledge and renew our obligations to obey him.

This was perfectly well understood by old *Anthony Albans*. Thou rememberest the sad accident which happened to him near us, by his being overturned in a road waggon, at the age of seventy-four. He was bruised and broken in a terrible manner, and it was thought he had but few hours to live. He had been accustomed to receive our Lord's Supper almost every month, for half an hundred years; and in this great extremity he expressed the most longing desires to perform this last duty to his crucified Lord. By the interposition of the good lady thy mistress, a clergyman was found; and Anthony, with all the sincerity of a dying man, was prepared for eternity. By the mercy of God, and by means of that lady's charity and pious kindness, he recovered. His temperance, and the calmness of his affection, were apparently instrumental to his cure, but perhaps not so much so as the calmness of his mind, produced by his custom of testifying his faith in Christ, and the practice of obedience to God's laws. As soon as his surgeon permitted him to go abroad, Anthony repaired to the house of prayer, there to pour forth his soul in grateful thanksgivings for the mercies which he had received.

Anthony used to reason thus: " of all commands " is it not natural to lay the greatest stress upon
" those

"those which are given us by our friends a little before their death, especially if we really love them, and they particularly defire it to be done, in remembrance of them?" And who is our beſt friend? ſurely Chriſt who died for us—And do we not wiſh that Chriſt ſhould remember us when he cometh to gather together his faithful ſervants and take them to heaven? If, MARY, the lady whom thou art now going to ſerve, ſhould by an aſtoniſhing mark of her love and compaſſion for thee, preſerve thy life; ſnatch thee alſo from the grave, or but die herſelf in the attempt to do ſo.—Suppoſe likewiſe that ſhe were to leave thee a creditable maintenance, upon the condition of thy doing ſome particular act eaſily performed; wouldſt thou not do it? If thou didſt it not, would not thy conduct be ungrateful, dark as the regions below, whilſt thy folly was the deriſion of children? Thou wouldeſt loſe thy ſupport by a negligence which would plunge thee into poverty, and gain thee the character of a mad perſon or an idiot. And yet, alas! this is nearly the caſe of the negligent, in reſpect to the Sacrament of the Lord's Supper. What can thy miſtreſs, or any mortal do for thee? She may help to ſave thy life for a few days or years, and render it comfortable, whilſt it laſteth, and then all her kindneſs muſt end: but *Chriſt* has promiſed a crown of everlaſting glory to all his faithful followers!

As to the matter which frightens ſo many people, the danger of eating and drinking unworthily, it ſtands thus. St. *Paul* reminds the *Corinthians*, that as they had *houses to eat and drink in*, they should not come to the house of God and to the Lord's Supper, without distinguishing a solemn act of religion, from a common meal, which was the crime of some of them. Well might he tell them, this was eating and drinking their own condemnation; which he explains by saying, that God would be provoked to inflict several kinds of judgments upon them, *if they continued to act so wicked a part*. But what is this to the purpose of those childish and fantastical fears, which a great part of us entertain in relation to the celebration of this act of devotion? Solemn indeed it is, and aweful; but when we fall down on our knees before God, or send up our hearts to him in prayer, is not this also a solemn and aweful duty?

As well may we say, that we will never pray, because it requires thought and seriousness, as to say that we will not receive the sacrament, because it requires thought and seriousness, and we may offend God if we are careless. We offend him most surely *by our not receiving*. And if we are to go to the table of our Lord in charity with all men, with an intention to lead a new life; can we do a greater good to our own souls than to go? In prayer we implore the mercies of heaven, upon the terms and conditions of forgiving others; which is far from being a hard task. And as we are always supposed to mean to repent, if we repent we amend: why then give up this part of our duty?

Let

Let the foolish world consider the Lord's-prayer: they will be astonished how they could live so long in neglect of the sacrament, and yet say this prayer once or twice every day of their lives! They pray that the will of God may be done on earth as it is in heaven, yet in this particular they regard not his *express* command: but do thou, my child, wait on the Lord, and keep his way.

In respect to the frequency of receiving, there is no time exactly pointed out. The doing it frequently seems to be implied, by the words of our Saviour, " Do this as oft as ye drink it in remembrance of me," Custom and consideration for the labour of the clergy may restrain some well meaning people from receiving often, but for my own part, I see not how any christian can decently turn his back on the Lord's table. The primitive christians received continually when they met.

Thou hast received the sacrament more than once; for heaven's sake, my child, *go on!* I know too well that *servants* are generally extremely remiss in this duty: A very honest domestic once asked me, on occasion of my expostulation, " Lord Sir, would you have me go among gentlemen;" as if he had conceived that the duty extended only to the higher classes; surely he was very little acquainted with the new testament and the history of our Saviour, and his disciples. The whole dispensation of the gospel confounds all human grandeur, when set in competition with an humble and contrite heart.

This

This poor man was convinced by my arguments, and acted like a *christian*.

If it should be the case with thy fellow-servants, I charge thee, as thou lovest the name of Christ, and hopest for mercy through his blood and sufferings, that thou followest not their example in negligence, but strivest to induce them to follow thine; and by discharging their obligation, promote their own safety and happiness. Bid them read the communion service with attention, and examine what the thing is before they condemn it, or in effect condemn themselves. If they are scrupulous, let them also read Dr. SYNGE's *excuses for not receiving the sacrament, answered.* And in regard to thyself, tell them what *thy father* said to thee at parting——— Remind them of the gross absurdity of supposing themselves wiser than the wisest, or more prudent than the soberest and best of mankind: let them consider whether the destruction which waits on the despisers of religion, be better than peace, and confidence in the mercies of God, and hope in everlasting joy. Remind them that they are as answerable to God for their neglect, as any other christian of the first rank and condition. The difference in situation is out of the question, where there is opportunity. We who move in a lower line of life have actually fewer temptations than people who are rich; and though we know less, we know so much that ignorance cannot be admitted as a plea.

If thy companions should not be awed by thy seriousness in this matter, but deride thee as a young saint,

saint, thou art not to reproach them, as if they were the contrary to young saints, but be patient and go on in the way thou art perſuaded is right; and mourn over their fooliſhneſs and obſtinacy: ſome of them perhaps would ſhut their eyes, if all the terrors of deſtruction ſtood in array before them, and opened wide their tremendous jaws.

Do thy duty, I ſay, and ſtill hope that others will do theirs. Thus thou wilt approve thyſelf worthy, and in good time receive thy reward. What canſt thou do more than expreſs thy ſorrow on this, as on all other occaſions, in which men tranſgreſs and rebel againſt common ſenſe, as well as the decrees of heaven?

Faith is reaſon improved by grace. In examining *Archbiſhop Synge's* inſtructions thou ſeeſt how *reaſon* and *faith* correſpond with a virtuous and religious life; and let nothing in thoſe inſtructions frighten thee, more than thou would'ſt be afraid of *virtue*, inſtead of being afraid of *vice*. I hope thou wilt be true to thyſelf, which is the way not to be falſe to thy God, or to thy fellow-creatures. " Humble thyſelf before God, and he will lift thee up. Quit thyſelf manfully, be ſtrong. A ſound heart is the life of the fleſh" and ſpirit.

DISCOURSE VIII.

The mistress's esteem for her servants agreeable to her steady principle in religion. Honesty in servants with a prudent conduct. The discretion of masters and mistresses essential to domestic peace. Character of an admirable female servant. Humility necessary in all stations.

THOU seest, my daughter, how much I interest myself in thy happiness upon the steady principles of a rational and religious conduct. I hope thou wilt value the present which I have made thee. The Lady thy mistress will not be displeased when she casts her eye on these exercises, nor will she despise them because they come from me, but judge freely of the author's performance as intended for use: perhaps her curiosity may be the more excited to read and meditate. It will not seem strange to her, who has a generous and liberal mind, that a christian, and a tender father, should spend some leisure hours in collecting and composing a few pious Invocations to heaven, such as I have reason to believe will be pleasing to a child whom he loves, and on whose virtues they will be well bestowed.

God knows what I shall be able to do for thee, in point of provision after my death. We who depend on the blessing of God on our honest labours, leave our children with the same kind of riches.
Thou

Thou art a child of providence in a distinguished manner. Trust to the goodness of it, using the means which providence has so visibly pointed out for thy support. Rejoice always under the care of heaven; and never expect to be happy from any thing the world can give thee, independant of thy hopes in a life to come.

The connexion between thy mistress and thee, is a solemn contract for mutual benefit, which ought to be held sacred; and it is necessary each should be informed, and truly understand what the other requires; that the discharge of this obligation with candour and justice, may create mutual kindness and regard.

Much must be submitted to in a state of servitude, but upon the whole it falls short in toil and danger of many other conditions.

In some countries servants are treated as slaves: but in Britain we are all free, and our treatment is suited to our liberty. Some masters however have a propensity to tyranny, and some servants are as much inclined to insolence and disobedience: but this proves nothing more than that there are foolish and bad people *in all conditions*; and that the good ought to be the more careful and vigilant in the exertion of those social virtues, on which their own peace and the general benefit of mankind so much depends.

Thy first thought should be, not to put thy mistress to any unnecessary expences; yet nothing can be a greater temptation to this, than the very reason that

that makes moſt againſt it; namely, the careleſsneſs or ignorance of a maſter or miſtreſs, which renders them ſubject to become a prey.

Let me charge thee to be ſtrictly on thy guard, to take no advantage, or do any thing unjuſtifiable, becauſe thou may'ſt perhaps be able to do it and not be diſcovered. Fraud in this caſe would be an aggravation of guilt; a cruelty added to injuſtice; and treachery to infidelity: and thoſe who take unwarrantable liberties in ſmall concerns, may be the more eaſily betrayed into great offences.

There are ſome families whoſe maſter or miſtreſs know not what their income, or expence is; they are hurried on by cuſtom and habit, and at length live in perpetual diſtreſs, for want of the means of ſuch a ſupply, as is neceſſary to put them on a level with thoſe who are their moſt conſtant companions.

Little doſt thou know of the anxiety which attends the condition of many a maſter and miſtreſs, to ſupport their rank, in the maintenance of their ſervants: Thou would'ſt not envy them, if thou could'ſt ſee their hearts. As a faithful ſervant, rejoice to ſee thy miſtreſs prudent, though thou mighteſt benefit more by her being extravagant.

Thou wouldeſt be aſtoniſhed, my child, if I were to relate to thee a quarter part of what I know, in relation to the devaſtation of people's fortunes, particularly by gaming, or in keeping more ſervants than they can afford; or by leaving things entirely to their management. As to gaming, it is a kind of inſanity: It is quarrelling with ourſelves: it is

an

an attempt to make ourselves miserable. As to servants that play for money, they ought to be considered as dangerous.

If thou shouldest become an upper servant, or act in any capacity of trust, be equally just and exact. Nor from a notion of charity suffer even the poor to be fed from the table of thy mistress without her leave. Look upon every penny of her money to be sacred; and touch not a farthing for thine own use, though thou shouldest mean to replace it. Set down what thou receivest immediately on the spot; and commit to writing what thou art paying, even before the money is out of thine hand. Do not trust thy memory, as some do, lest thou should'st lose thy money, or be tempted to charge at random.

In regard to honesty, thou canst not be too scrupulously strict.—*William Stitch* found in the pocket of a Lord Noble's waistcoat, which had been put into his hands to new button, a bank note of an hundred pounds. *William* brought it home, and desired to see my Lord; and being admitted into his presence, told him what he had found, and that he did not chuse to deliver it to any one but his Lordship. My Lord commended his honesty, and desired *William* to accept of *five guineas.*—" What, my Lord," says he, " take money for being honest! no: the satisfaction of my own mind in doing my duty is a reward, that abundantly repays me. God forbid that I should be ever tempted to withhold another man's right, or expect a reward for doing him justice?"

Carry

Carry this in thy mind, that as *good masters and mistresses* generally make *good servants*, so good servants not only preserve the tranquility of families, but frequently are the means of saving them from ruin. My master once told me of a friend of his, who was obliged by misfortunes to contract his expences: he had given credit to some of his acquaintance, who violated the most sacred ties of confidence, and left him in distress. In this situation he was obliged, in his old age, to discharge all his domestics. Servants are generally acquainted with their master's circumstances. This gentleman indeed made no secret of his: he told his servants why he paid them off. One of them, whose name was Theodosia Hope, burst into tears, and said to him: " Sir, I have been your cook five and twenty years, I have always honoured and respected you; you have treated me with the greatest kindness as a master, a father, and a friend. I have been saving, that I might neither die for want, nor depend upon my parish for a support; and I have laid by some scores of pounds; but I can never live in peace whilst I think that you are in any kind of distress. To you, under the good care of providence, I owe my life: to you I am indebted for much good instruction, for the safety of my soul; I beg you will accept of my purse, and all it contains: it is the bounty of heaven; and in heaven I trust. He that feedeth the ravens, and letteth not a sparrow fall unheeded to the ground, will not forsake *me*. I am yet able to work; suffer me to attend your fortunes, and be your

your servant still! Perhaps you may not find another so faithful and affectionate!" *Theodosia* drew tears from her good old master; he was not too proud to weep at the generosity of his servant: her offer of continuing with him was accepted. Not long after a relation of his left him a considerable fortune; and when he died, he bequeathed a very comfortable maintenance to his faithful cook-maid.

Theodosia's mother also was an excellent woman; she lived to the uncommon age of 101.

This character of her is engraved upon a stone in Bromley church-yard, in Kent.

> Let it be remembered
> That there is no station in which industry
> Will not obtain power to be liberal;
> Nor any character on which liberality
> Will not confer honour.
> She had been long prepared
> By a simple and unaffected piety,
> For that aweful moment,
> Which however delayed, is universally sure.
> How few are allowed an equal time of probation!
> How many by their lives presume upon more!
> To perpetuate the memory of this person,
> But yet more, to perpetuate the lesson of her life,
> By voluntary contributions
> This stone was erected.

If a servant is capable of the duty required, and the master not tyrannical, neither of them will be disturbed by little incidents. Each will make a candid

candid allowance for the other's frailties. If master and servant dislike each other, or a servant is really unfit for a place, let them part with good wishes for their mutual prosperity.

Humility is a virtue required in all stations, but a proud servant, is a most inconsistent character. Pride and vanity lead to the depths of distress. Half the wretched beings of thy sex, who live on the deplorable wages of iniquity, for the short time they live at all, owe their being discharged out of service, to *pride*.

Submission is another branch of humility. St. Peter recommends to us, with the force of the divine commandment, " Servants be subject to your " masters, with all fear, not only to the good and " gentle, but also to the froward: for this is thank- " worthy, if a man, for conscience toward God, " endure grief, suffering wrongfully. For what " glory is it, if when ye be buffeted for your faults, " ye shall take it patiently? But if when ye do well " and suffer for it, ye take it patiently, this is ac- " ceptable with God." It is also said, that " it is " good for a man that he bear the yoke in his " youth." He had indeed better be tried, and learn patience in his early days, than in advanced years.

There are cases in which it is necessary " the knee " should bow though the understanding cannot." This depends on the prudence of a servant, as well as his comprehension of the true nature of his situation. Always consider calmly what the evil is,

and

and what the remedy may be. "He that shoots at the stars may hurt himself, but cannot endanger them." A master or a mistress may admonish once or twice, or thrice, but a continued repetition of the same faults or inadvertencies, will tire out the most patient.

My master was of a quick temper, and sometimes said what he might as well have omitted: but he was of a humane, friendly, and pious disposition, and generally corrected himself. He overlooked many of my faults, and therefore I was the more patient under his. If thy mistress is of a *lively, quick temper*, thou wilt often think her *impatient*, though she should have the *patience* to tell thee ten times, of the same fault: but I charge thee to beware of impatience, lest thou should'st make a pert reply, and at once shew thyself *ill-mannered* and *ungrateful*, and ruin thyself in her favour.

My advice is, that instead of resenting, thou should'st learn to *compassionate:* Do not imagine, that mercy and compassion were made to be exercised only by the great and wealthy towards inferiors; the *rich* and *powerful* themselves are frequently as great objects of pity, as those who beg their bread. By no means pretend to be as wise as thy mistress: If there should be good reason for believing thyself to be in the right, and she in the wrong, yet remember how much the chance is against thee, not only from thy want of age and experience, but from the lowness of thy education,
and

and the want of those means of obtaining knowledge which she has enjoyed.

Above all things avoid expostulation with thy mistress. It is too common a practice with passionate persons, when reproached, to tell masters and mistresses that they understand their business, forgetting that the question is on the article of obedience. Consider what thou mayest lose, and how improbable it is thou shouldest gain any thing by pert replies, and the gratification of *talking*. No master or mistress of spirit, will bear to be flatly contradicted by a servant, or to argue with them about indifferent matters.

In cases wherein thy virtue is not hurt, their pleasure should be thy law, never forgetting any thing that materially affects their interest. If any difficulty arises in matters of fact, there is an humble way of asking leave to acquaint them how the case really stands.

If thou art accused of any thing, as a fault, which thou really thinkest to be such, the honest confession is the surest way of obtaining pardon.

It is good policy to observe attentively the temper a party is in, at a time when accidents happen. Use thy discretion in all things; forget not to avoid whatever has the appearances of sullenness, and make ready and direct answers, to the best of thy knowledge and belief, looking calmly at the person thou art speaking to.

DISCOURSE IX.

Danger of servants on changing places. The conduct of favourites towards fellow-servants. Behaviour of mistresses. Civility. Cleanliness. Caution against fire.

IT is common with servants to entertain each other, with accounts of *profitable places;* and how much wages some have more than others. They do not consider so much the comfort and peace, the safety, and good treatment they enjoy, as how much they may get; I say *may* get, for it is not the lot of one in a thousand to gain such services as are represented to them; nor perhaps to have abilities to keep such places, if they do gain them. Servants are apt to judge of the best places, as people do of the highest prize in a lottery; and in hunting after an imaginary advantage, they often plunge themselves into real distress. Let me advise thee, MARY, to be contented, and *learn when thou art well,* and not desire to be *better* than well. If thou findest good treatment, let this be considered as superior in value to any such additional wages, as thou mightest have the fortune to obtain. In thy situation, as a young woman, a fondness for change can hardly fail to produce mischief. I do not say but that in due time thou mayest reasonably expect an increase of wages.

If thou should'ft become a favorite, employ thy influence to keep peace in the family. Make open profeffion of thy refolution, at once to be true to thy miftrefs, but not the lefs friendly to thy fellow-fervants, when they do their duty.

In all matters of difficulty apply to thy miftrefs, and entreat of her to decide for thee. Favourites are generally more feared than loved; and more intrigues are formed to enfnare them, than thou canft fufpect. Our good qualities often expofe us to more hatred and perfecution than all the evil we do; and yet it is not the lefs true, that " honefty is the beft policy." Truth will prevail in the end; and it is thy duty to do the beft thou canft, fairly and honeftly, to promote thine own welfare.

If unhappily any of thy fellow-fervants are remifs in their duty, remind them of it in civil and obliging terms. If they will not take thy advice, thou haft neverthelefs difcharged thy part. When evil confequences enfue from their not regarding thee, do not aggravate their misfortunes by taunts and reproaches, as weak-minded people fometimes do. All that fhould be faid is, " *I wifh you had been of my opinion.*" Soft words and ready anfwers, with an open ingenuoufnefs, have power to calm the moft perverfe minds.

If thou thinkeft any fellow-fervant as well inclined as thyfelf, be her friend; but from the moment fhe is guilty of any fraud or injuftice, or entertains thee with difcourfe againft the perfon whofe bread thou art eating, thou mayeft fufpect, that fhe

is

is not found at heart: she is ignorant or perverse. It should be thy part to soften such discourse, and palliate the real faults, much more the foibles of thy mistress: but if thou condemnest her when she is blameless, thou art guilty of injustice as well as ingratitude.

Thou wilt generally find that those who complain most of others, are most blameable themselves. Reason calmly with them. Advise them to consider the condition of their service, to represent their grievances, not to condemn their judge, before they appeal to him for justice. If servants have a sense of religion on their mind they will " hate vain thoughts, and love the law of God."

As I have the happiness to be known to the lady who will take thee, MARY, as a servant, I promise myself it will be so much the better for thee, if thou art not wanting to thyself.

She will probably tell thee, " she knows thy father to be an honest man; and that she hath a respect for him; and if thou art a true daughter of his, that thou wilt be a faithful and good servant to her; and if thy conduct sheweth that thou art, thou mayest be assured of her friendship." Now, my child, if thou should'st set out with such prepossessions in thy favour, it will be a happy omen of success: but at all events take thy lot.

There are some people whose thoughts are so dissipated, that one must repeat the same words before they are awake enough to know what is said to them. This is a great unhappiness, and very irksome to a master or mistress, but it is not altogether incurable; for if the servant has any delight in doing her duty, she will be attentive to the commands, to which she is bound by every tie, to be obedient.———One thing necessary to awaken attention, is to *look at the person who is speaking to thee*. The countenance demands respect, and helps the understanding; and seeing the motion of another's lips, assists the hearing, whereas the want of this kind of attention, is ill-mannered, even among equals, and much more from a servant.

Always take the first opportunity of mentioning what is necessary, particularly in cases wherein thou hast been commanded to do any thing, or hast received any message. Take it for granted that thy mistress will not be informed of what relates to her interest and thy own duty, unless thou tellest her; and consider it as injustice and a breach of duty, to keep her in ignorance.

If thy memory be treacherous, keep a memorandum-book, and by one act of recollection, which is to look into thy book, thou mayest be sure that nothing will be omitted.

Memory depends on the exercise of it. Experience must teach what confidence to place in thy own, and what assistances are necessary to it. To plead forgetfulness, when thou art paid for remembering, is but a sad excuse; and if it happens often will render thee unworthy of thy service.

Never put off any business to a distant hour; but perform what thou canst immediately. Take care

not

not to shuffle nor equivocate upon being accused of negligence. The more conscious thou art of neglect, the more thou should'st beg pardon. But all pretences, such as *I thought this or that*, when in truth thou didst not think at all, are abominable in the sight of God.

Dirt and filthiness fall within the observation of every one; and neatness and cleanliness, like comeliness in person, is a silent recommendation. These are to the body, what purity is to the soul. Every young woman of sentiment naturally aspires at making a cleanly appearance.

The decent and cleanly carry with them a presumptive proof of a virtuous disposition. *Industry* is generally the companion of *cleanliness*. A cleanly beggar engages much higher attention than a dirty one. Consider what is proper to thy condition, rather erring on the cleanly side: a slovenly *good* servant, of either sex, is a contradiction.

Let me warn thee of the many fatal accidents which happen by fire; nine in ten of these are the effects of carelessness in servants; either from their being in liquor, from their gross ignorance, or unpardonable thoughtlessness. I charge thee to consider, MARY, what misfortunes and miseries may be brought upon others by fire, which is so admirable a servant, and so terrible a master. Pestilence, sword and famine, do not make such sudden and outrageous havock as this element.

I have been sometimes astonished at the carelessness of my fellow-servants, in leaving candles lighted where they should have been extinguished; and carrying them about with long wicks, even so as to drop fire, and sometimes holding them near linen, or other combustible matter: it was my master's rule to order his candles for common use, to be only of half the length of the ordinary size; and to use flat candlesticks of at least 12 inches diameter, and 3 inches high in the socket; with snuffers and extinguisher hung to the socket. He likewise gave strict orders not to leave chimneys too long unswept.—Not to burn papers, or by any other way to make a great blaze in the fire-place.—Not to leave a drawing-stove covered.—Not to leave a poker in the fire.—Not to leave a candle burning in a room.—Not to leave linen airing near a fire unwatched.—Not to carry a lighted candle into a closet.—Not to be any way busy with a candle where there was linen or paper.—Not to carry a candle into a stable without a lanthorn.—Not to venture even the lanthorn and candle in a hay-loft.—And where the floor of any room was grown spungy, and combustible by age, to keep the part so affected covered with something woollen, lest a spark should fall on it from a candle. In going to bed, we were desired to use a short candle and a large flat candlestick, taking care in both cases never to be without an extinguisher: and not to bring a lighted candle near a bed. These are rules which I recommend to thee, my dear child, to be observed, as thou regardest thy duty to God, and thy neighbour; and as thou meanest to avoid the punishment which the

laws

laws of the land inflict on the careless as well as wilful, which is, to suffer imprisonment, 'till one hundred pounds penalty be paid for a careless deed; a wilful one is death by the laws of our country.

DISCOURSE X.

The advantages of temperance. Propriety in the dress of servants. Danger of crouded meetings. Effects of the undistinguished use of tea.

TEMPERANCE, my dear child, is the friend to reason, the companion of religion, the offspring of virtue, and the parent of health. The wise man says, "Sound sleep cometh of moderate "eating, he riseth early and his wits are about him; "but the pains of watching and choler, and pangs "of the belly, are with an insatiable man." Nature is relieved by a little good food taken in time, and we grow strong and healthy: but eating above measure destroys health, wounds peace, and banishes comfort from our hearts.

Many act as if eating were their highest bliss. Regard not thy taste above measure; but acquire a habit of indifference in respect to the quality of food: hunger will relish the plainest.

Daintiness in diet, in people of fortune, makes them contemptible. But when servants are dainty, and not contented with common food, they betray their depraved inclinations, and become a nuisance to a family. High-cooked dishes are poisonous; they inflame the blood: SOLOMON's advice is, " eat " as becometh thee, such things are set before thee, " and devour not, left thou be hated." Consult the pleasure of others as well as thine own, and be not impatient to seize thy food, nor eat it faster than is decent and wholesome. In general we eat much *too fast*, and this acts doubly against us, for by such means we are the more easily betrayed into eating *too much*.

Beer is our common liquor, and when good in its kind, is excellent for those who work hard; but the pure element which nature affords, being likewise good of its kind, is the grand medicine as well as aliment of life.

I have learnt by experience that water is the best preservative from diseases: but people may drown their bowels by drinking too much of it. Even bad water may be rendered wholesome by boiling and infusing herbs of our own growth *.

Servants run mad almost about tea; they spend a great portion of their wages in it, and squander too much of their time, in this kind of tipling, I can give it no better name.

* Ground ivy, mint, sage, or rosemary, being dried and infused in boiling water, and drank cold, commonly called herb tea, is incomparably better than bad small-beer which the poor often drink; and they would esteem it, but that the herbs are not properly gathered and dried, and the infusion is usually made too strong. I am now supposing places where water is not good: but in England we are for the most part happy in this particular.

The poor are stupidly insensible, how they are gall'd in their health either by the bad sort of tea which they often drink; by the habit of sipping, instead of drinking; by using so much hot liquor, when cold would answer better to invigorate them; they consider not how they injure themselves and families by consuming a large portion of their time; and of the money which they gain by hard labour. How much wiser would it be to spend their money in substantial and nourishing food!

The article of butter, which our forefathers used to eat only as a dainty, is becoming a necessary of addition to tea drinking, and our dairies give so much the less cheese and good milk porridge.

Servants, like other people, have certainly a right to their share of the improvements which time and riches, skill and industry have made. But I am afraid, MARY, we often travel too fast. Young women in service dress too much like their mistresses, which gives them a wrong turn. If thy mistress should give thee any of her left off clothes, consider what is proper for thee to wear, and in what shape; and dispose of the rest.

Let me warn thee also against the deadly effect of air, when rendered corrupt by too many people being assembled, or by being too much confined.

My dear child, avoid *shows* in close places, and all such entertainments, as are not worth the hazard of health to any body in their senses. Health to the body is as virtue to the soul. It is often squandered away in the most foolish manner imaginable, beauty cherishing its own bane. Let me also advise you to let air freely into all the rooms under your care; do not mind a little trouble in opening and shutting windows, for the health of people greatly depends upon their having their apartments well aired.

DISCOURSE XI.

Character of the mistress. Her charity, punctuality, dislike of cards, calmness of temper, religious chearfulness, &c.

WHILE thou takest care of thy health, as far as thy duty and calling admit, remember that a truly rational and religious conduct always makes those who are most distinguished appear *singular:* people who are of a contrary character, or do not understand on what principle their neighbour acts, are apt to reproach wantonly, as if there were some capital defect in not conforming in all points to the world. The lady thou art going to serve is called a *very particular woman:* The truth is, that she has so much religion, as not to be satisfied without prayers in her family every morning and every night, and all her servants attend. On the Sunday evening, she, or some of her friends who visit her, reads a sermon. She acts as if she counted the days and nights, and numbered them so far as really to apply her heart unto wisdom. It is upon the same principle this lady requires all her servants to go to church,

church, either in the morning or evening, every sabbath-day: and she absolutely will not keep any servant who totally declines going to the Sacrament of our Lord's Supper: she does not declare this in so many words; but if repeated admonitions, and the most pious, humane, and friendly advice make no impression, she discharges them. She will be attended by those she calls *christians* on whom she can depend.

In order to keep her servants virtuous, this lady keeps them *employed*, giving them this wholesome admonition; " Get thy *spindle* and thy *distaff* ready, " and *God* will send thee *flax*," adding this proverb, "*Think* of ease, but work on;" supposing that *ease* is the object which all mankind are naturally inclined to *seek*, though they find true pleasure only in *action*.

Thy mistress has all the tenderness of a woman, without the foibles usually attending thy sex: her *charity* flows from her *religion*, and is cherished by the *compassion* which streams from her heart, and is therefore steady and lasting. She judges always on the *merciful side*, distinguishing *faults* from *crimes*; and considers the condition servants are in, as well as the kind of education they have had. All who ever served her, and have not been guilty in such a manner as to render them unworthy of her confidence, are sure of her good word as far as she can give it with a *safe conscience*; but she never will give a good character of a servant who has no title to it, declaring that she considers deceit in recommending servants out of mere compassion, and against truth, as *robbing* in order to give alms to the poor.

What thinkest thou of the gentleman, who notwithstanding he knew his servant had robbed him, recommended him to another master? The consequence was that he robbed *him* also; upon which he prosecuted the former master, who was accordingly condemned to *pay the loss*, and should moreover have been fined.

Thy mistress is exact in money matters, and makes up her accounts every monday morning, paying *ready money* for every thing she buys: by this means she lives elegantly and splendidly, with *half*, or at the most *two-thirds* of the sum, which those spend who would never pay their debts at all, if they could cut off the long arms of the law. Her maxim in this respect is, " better go to bed supperless, than rise in debt;" intimating that many charges are contracted by purchasing things which are not *necessary*: and that some necessary things should be given up, rather than run in debt for them.

This lady dresses according to her fortune, but she confines herself to a certain moderate sum yearly, expending more in deeds of charity than in her apparel.

Thou art also to understand that thy mistress dislikes cards, yet not so but she will play for an hour, to oblige her friends, in a private family.

Instead of spending her time in gaming as too many persons of fortune do, this lady's chief delight, is in promoting the welfare of her fellow-creatures, as far as she can extend her power. She is temperate in her diet, and remarkable in keeping good hours, paying for none of her amusements more than they are worth.

Though she appears to have great sensibility, and is naturally of a quick temper, she speaks calmly, and has acquired such a command of her passions, that she seems to weep or rejoice, only as a just sense of things drawn from thought and experience, have taught her. She has seen and felt what it is to be unfortunate, and says that "no one knows better what *good* is, than he who hath endured *evil*."

The consciousness that she is endeavouring to pass her time on earth, agreeably to the design of heaven, gives a peculiar chearfulness and sweetness to her manners.

She often talks of death, as the end of her days, and of her cares; and wonders to see such a bustle among people who have already one foot in the grave. She speaks of her dissolution in so familiar and unaffected a manner, that no one can doubt of her being perfectly reconciled to the will of heaven. Art thou not charmed, my dear, with the character of thy mistress? Endeavour to imitate it then, for whatever our fortune and condition may be, my child, we may all cultivate the same sentiments, and by degrees acquire *the same happy turn of mind*. By serving her truly and faithfully, thou wilt in the end serve thyself, though she should not in all respects perfectly answer my report.

DISCOURSE XII.

Reflections on the vicissitudes of human life. The sorrows it is subject to, and the liberality of nature in affording us comfort.

MUCH have I to say to thee on the various events to which our condition is subject, the evils against which we are to guard in our christian warfare, and how to conduct ourselves under them.

Thou knowest that I married the woman I loved beyond all others in the world. For awhile nothing seemed to be wanting to complete my happiness, and when thou, my child, camest into the world, my fancy represented to me that thou would'st prove so good I should have no reason to envy the greatest of mankind. Thy mother became sickly. I sympathized in her pains and sorrows; and all the beautiful structure of my happiness was thrown down and blown away, like the dust of which I am made. Soon after her death, I lost my two little boys, your brothers. In my fancy they still hang round my neck, and in their charming images, live in my heart! Heaven delivered *them* from ever suffering such sorrows! Then fell my good old master! His last kind words still sound in my ears:—it is true he made a provision for me, but I loved and honoured him so much, that I suffered more anguish at his death, than joy at his liberality. Indeed his kindness

ness added to my grief. These sorrows, and some or other such all must expect, threw a cloud over my brightest days! Such however has been the goodness of God, through Jesus Christ, that he has enabled me to become in all things resigned to his will. God never afflicts his creatures but for their good; and I have, by degrees, attained such a peaceful serenity of mind, such a freedom from undue anxiety, as the world and its pursuits can never give!

In this point of view, I rejoice: every part of nature furnishes me with matter for delight and gratitude! The grass that grows in the fields; the leaves which shoot from the trees, and the fruit which they furnish; the growth of every plant, and every animal, is full of wonder! Where wilt thou find the hand of art, which can give the cowslip such a yellow, or the violet such a blue? Hast thou considered how beautifully the rose is adorned, and how justly it is the emblem of the most captivating charms of female beauty! Nor is the apple or the peach less grateful to the eye. Have not thy senses been often refreshed with the smell of new hay, and the sweet fragrance of herbs and flowers, and the blossoms of trees!

Nor is it only in the vegetable world;—the bleating flock furnishes wool for the employment of many thousands, who again provide cloathing for millions more. This makes me think myself of some importance; and when I see the *ruddy lass*, drawing streams of milk from the swelled udder of

the

the *useful cow*, methinks I am the instrument of heaven, in rearing the tender helpless infant, whilst the drooping grandfather blesses the hand that brings him milk.

Survey the multitude of objects which providence certainly intends for delight as well as use. When I behold thee feeding my poultry and my pigeons, I think that if a sparrow falleth not to the ground, but by the knowledge and permission of the God of all, he has honoured thee as the instrument of his bounty, in feeding these birds which are so useful to mankind!—And if SOLOMON, in all his glory, was not arrayed like a lilly of the field, what dost thou think of the natural beauty of the splendid feathers of the strutting peacock, or the scarlet ornament of the prouder turkey?—These are alike the work of thy hands, O God supreme!—O my child, when thou hearest the early crowing of the cock, dost thou not think of him who calls thee to a vigilant and active life? If thou considerest not what business thou hast on thy hand to-day, perhaps to-morrow will never come to thee. This bird is thy friendly monitor.

It is here in the country we must enjoy the liberal feast which kind providence hath provided: here every tree, and every bush furnishes something to the common stock. We might live without great cities, but they could not subsist without husbandry. Nor do we barely live. See there the *fragrant bean*, and *pea* in blossom, furnish *pleasure* as well as
food;

food; whilst the chearful notes of birds on every tree fill the soul with gladness!

Is not this far beyond all the gay inventions of city entertainments, where health so often becomes a prey; where fraud and enmity are so frequently concealed under the garb of friendship and pretended love; and men, bewildering and bewildered, often seek happiness in paths which lead to misery? yet God knows, our vices here in the country are also too big to be overlooked. We are often vain and foolish, but pride and folly seem more contagious in great cities, where thou wilt find numbers who know not what to do with themselves, or have so little leisure from vain pursuits and empty joys, that they hardly afford themselves time to think what course is best to steer, to prevent intemperance and preserve their lives. As to things of real value, they see not how rapidly life ebbs out; the great business of salvation grows heavy in proportion to their neglect of it.

Some part of my days have been chiefly spent in the tumult and parade of great cities, where generally the worst, as well as the best part of a nation are assembled; and where vice is much easier propagated than virtue. In spite of all the silken robes, or lighted tapers which I have seen, or the melodious music I have heard, I never had so true a relish of life, as in the country. Often have I lamented the fate of my good master's friends. By meeting in such multitudes, they at once robbed themselves of two of the choicest of blessings, *pure air,*

air, and *time* for reflection, and shortened their lives.

I do not mean to depreciate masters or servants, who perhaps are much wiser and better than myself: but in order to give thee right notions of a city life in great families, I will tell thee that I form my judgment from the real conduct of people.

When I was in *service* I had many opportunities of making remarks: I often saw *interest, fancy, opinion*, and above all, *custom*, govern so much, and *reason* so little, that I hardly believed some people were rational creatures.—But let nothing dismay thee, my child! for although *folly* will never be put out of countenance whilst there are so many unwise people in the world of all conditions; yet *wisdom* will always be justified of her true children. What is right and fit for us, in our several stations in this world, considered as beings on our passage to eternity, will still be right and fit; and the good will find such countenance in the world, as is sufficient for their purpose.

Thou must take thy lot: Gladly would I retain thee, as my partner in my toils and comforts as a farmer, and lead thee through the dangerous paths of life, had it not pleased heaven to present so excellent a lady to thee for a mistress. I hope she will be a guide, a teacher, and a friend. Alas! my child, there are not many such, nor many servants who know *when they are well*; or consider that state of servitude, wherein their morals and piety are most attended to, as the *best place* they can be in. Which

soever

soever way I turn my thoughts, I discover danger. Wert thou put out apprentice in some great city, to an useful trade, with a view to a superior fortune, I know the world so well, thou would'st be more exposed than in a well regulated private family. Think of the instruction thou hast received, and I trust thou wilt be safe. Use the means which God hath given thee, he will be thy friend and thy defender!

DISCOURSE XIII.

Thoughts on the importance of time. Calculation of the probable duration of life. Thoughts on death.

AS Providence seems determined that we must part, let us improve every hour that remaineth, before the day comes; and hear me, O my child, with deep attention! Whether in sorrow, or in joy; in good fortune, or in bad; death ere long will separate us. Thou perchance wilt go to the land where all things are forgotten, before thou thinkest of it: *I must go soon!* Let us both prepare for that journey, as the last thing which we shall have to do. I need not tell thee, that even these transient minutes of our discourse, which I pass with so much pleasure in thy company, bring us so much the nearer to our end.

In the great view of immortality, what advantage can there be in living, but as we *improve our time?* Those days are lost in which we do no good; and worse than lost, when we do evil. Whether alone, or in company, we must be provident of our time! We had better not live, than have bad thoughts, or spend our time in bad company. Those who seek for amusements, which are either foolish or wicked, with a view to what they call killing of time, consider but little what a sad compliment they make to a guest, whom, though we should court with all the smiles of love, and all the tenderness and respect of friendship, is ever on the wing. There is no occasion to murder him to get quit of him. *Yesterday* is already dead; *to-morrow* is not yet born; what have we then except *to-day?* and shall one poor day create such distress, to make us think of murdering our best friend? How quickly fly the hours from morn to noon, and from noon to night; and then we fall into the arms of sleep, which is the image of death! How monstrous it is to treat with disrespect the best friend we have in the world. This is the case with those who abuse that reverend personage, *Time.*

Let me charge thee, as thou lovest thy tender father, to remember how difficult it is to be innocent and idle. If thou seekest to be happy, be industrious! Is any thing more certain, than that those who are properly *idle people,* are more troubled and perplexed what to do with their time, than the industrious can possibly be on account of the hardest labour

labour they perform. The hardest task is to support ourselves having nothing to do. This is for the honour of *industry!* But it goes much further: it proves the gracious design of providence, by putting the rich and poor more upon an equality than either of them generally imagine. The poor fill up their time with work, such as is useful to themselves and the rest of mankind; and the rich, such as are not industrious, nor employed in useful occupations, are perpetually laying out what to do with to-morrow, and continually labouring in thought, by what means they shall fill up their time: they think they have a vast superfluity, because they cannot tell what to do with it. It is probable such will repent, as many a rich prodigal hath done who has squandered a large fortune, and been reduced to poverty. Those who understand the value of *time,* treat it as prudent people do their money; instead of spending a great deal upon *nothing that is useful,* they make a little go a great way.

It is the right use and application of time, which not only makes life long, but renders it pleasant also; especially when we are brought to delight in doing the will of God.——What a shocking thing it is, to hear people complain, that their hours move heavily, when they should be working with their hands, or performing some duty of charity, reading some pious or useful book, or doing something that will make them wiser and better than they were before! They are sure the hour will come, when they may be glad to part with all the

wealth

wealth in the world, were they poffeffed of it, in exchange for a fingle day.

Thofe who are much captivated with this world, of either fex, being averfe to the thoughts of parting with it, generally reckon upon *years*, and are often furprized. They banifh the thoughts of death, by confidering him as if he were an enemy who will not come if he is not thought of: but this is far from being true: it often happens when his meffengers, ficknefs or age are at our doors, we do not ferioufly believe that he is coming. The reafon of this I apprehend to be, that he takes fuch a variety of forms, we cannot well diftinguifh him till we feel his dart; and therefore fo many make this a reafon for believing that he is always at a great diftance from them.

In the ordinary courfe of things, green fruit often falls by a blaft, or violence, or the various accidents to which it is fubject. This is the cafe of thofe who die in youth; but as fruit that is ripened by time, and its proper feafon, muft fall; fo the aged muft die. Death is the hufbandman that gathers us all in.

Perhaps it may adminifter to the eftablifhment of thy virtue, to know what I gathered from my mafter's books, when I was young, confirmed by my obfervation. Doft thou apprehend, that thy father is now trading on the laft fifth part of his ftock of life, as all men are who are paft fifty? * Thou

---

* Of 1000 born, 785 are dead by the age of 50, being very near 4 in 5.

seest me chearful and in good spirits, but nature, the great agent of the Almighty, has sentenced me to death. I am one in four who is to die in five years *. It is true, I do not know certainly, within five years of my death; but this I know, that if I should live through five years, then a greater proportion than one, in some other four, must die, as it were in my place.

And what think you, child, is your hazard? Hear, and be not discomfited! Your chance is near one in five to die in fifteen years †. Look round thee! see how swift the scythe of death mows down the children of men. Figure to thyself the procession of human life: observe the reality of what is passing before thine eyes: behold the rich and the poor; the wise and the foolish; the virtuous and the wicked; those who make much noise, and those who are never heard of, beyond the circle of their acquaintance; they all march on together to one common grave, which is always open, and never full!

Thou, though yet so young, must notwithstanding have observed how quickly infants pass into childhood; childhood into youth; youth into manhood; manhood into middle age; this again into what we call advanced years, and from thence how soon we appear in old age! This progression of life, to

---

* From 55 to 60, 38 in 173 die, which is near 1 in 4. From 63 to 74, 4 in 5 drop.

† This is founded on 502 of 15 years old: of these, by the time they reached 30, 94 were dead, so that it comes to near 1 in 5.

people of observation, appears amazingly quick Thou hearest it from every one's mouth; "Good God, is it possible! it seems to be but yesterday that such an one was a child!" It is possible, for the fact is really so.

The eldest, as well as the youngest of us, have designs and projects, hopes and expectations, which require time for the execution, perhaps beyond the chance of our continuance in life; but in many cases this is necessary, and promotes social good.

The folly and madness is, to live in sin, and defer repentance, at the very moment that we see some one of our acquaintance drop almost every day, at every age; 'and knowing, as we do, that our knell must toll like other people's.

What a bustle do we make about life, and how often forget the end and design of it? It is but a small object, a mere sun-beam playing in the air, disappearing as the light withdraws, to those who have solid hopes beyond the grave; it indeed presents a different view to them who have no such hopes, for these have fears that they shall be miserable.

Every distinct person flatters himself that he shall not be of the number of those who die early. Providence is indulgent to us: for though every day brings us nearer to our end, death never seems near: the hour being concealed from us, we enjoy this turn of mind, and suffer no fruitless pain.—O God, how manifest are thy mercy and goodness, in all thy conduct towards man!—Think of these, my dear child, and adore God with a grateful heart! Whether thou
shalt

shalt die young, or live to old age, remember, "that honourable age is not that which standeth in length of time, nor that which is measured by number of years; but wisdom is grey hairs unto men, and unspotted life is old age." The wise man means, *That* wisdom, which will teach thee to remember thy Creator in the days of thy youth, and to apply thy heart so diligently to please him, that he may receive thee into everlasting joy.

Let us be careful so to conduct ourselves, that we may not be disinherited for disobedience!—Learn from such considerations, how highly valuable thou art to thyself. The opportunity of knowledge will be increased after this life; but the only opportunity of doing good, *is now*. If thou takest care to improve this, thou art sufficiently secure of the other; but if this be neglected, all is lost. I have lived long: thou wishest to live long: I mean that thou should'st take advantage of my thoughts and experience; and now is thy age of learning. I feel and deplore my own unworthiness; and discover more of other men's, than it is possible for thee to do at thy age. Still I learn more and more; and above all, how unreasonable it would be to quarrel with others for being so much like myself. The longer I live, and the more I see of the world, the more I wean myself from it: This will, I hope, be thy case, when thou knowest as much of it as I do. In the mean time press forward, to be every day more wise, and more virtuous; and never tire in doing all the good thou canst, in spite of the folly and ingratitude thou wilt meet with. I have no flattering hopes that I shall ever reach the perfection which my mind aspires after; but it is my ambition, as I know it to be my glory, to press forward "toward the mark for the "prize of the high calling of God in *Christ Jesus!*"

DISCOURSE XIV.

The indispensible condition of happiness in the life to come. Deaths of many persons of distinguished characters under particular circumstances of repentance.

I DID not finish yesterday, all that I meant to say on the interesting subject we were then upon. Thou wilt probably see me soon, a lump of inanimate clay, and consequently, with respect to this world, all my thoughts perished: But thou hast the happiness, of knowing with full assurance, how God hath declared by the holy scriptures, that death shall open a passage to eternity; a blessed eternity to the good; though to the wicked an eternity of misery. Those are not properly *christians,* who do not believe in the promises made by *Jesus Christ.*

Keep thine eye continually on the judgment to come, as the only secure method of governing life by the rules of reason and religion. Think of the misery of not being able to look backward without shame, nor forward without terror. Think of that which will give thee comfort in the last extremity, for that last extremity will come, as surely as thou

now

now livest, there can be no evasion.—My prayer is, "Grant, O Father, and eternal God, that I may live the remainder of my days, whatever the number of them shall be, in thy fear and to thy glory; and let me die the death of the righteous. Farther I implore thy favour and mercy to my child, the dearest gift thou hast been pleased to bestow upon me, and whose life and manners I have endeavoured to form on this great principle, that holiness alone is acceptable in thy sight, and therefore the supreme good of mortals here below, in every station which thou hast assigned them. This petition I offer at thy throne, O God, in the name of thy son Jesus Christ!"

It may, with the greatest reason, be asked of any one, who trembles at the thought of death, or who is enamoured with the love of life, what is it that thou valuest life for? Is it for riches?—these often make themselves wings, and oftener prove the more immediate causes of disease of body, and anguish of mind. They frequently create more cares than extreme poverty produces.—Is it for honours? these fade at the frown of princes, and as often, at the capricious applause of the people. Happy for such as you and I, evils of this kind cannot reach us.—Is it for beauty? this falls not to the lot of many, and often proves the parent of misfortune; and it is true, even to a proverb, whatever good or evil beauty hath occasioned, it is but as a flower that withers away. —Is it health that enchanteth thee? This is a blessing indeed, but it is subject to change, and the strength which attends it always abates as life draws to its close.

Let it be the rule of thy life, to make up thy accounts every night. Consider, my child, what thou hast *said* and *done*; nor let thy *thoughts* go unchastised. Thus wilt thou be able to state thy reckoning fairly; and "if thy sins die before thee, thou "wilt have nothing to do, when death comes,— "but to die!"

It is natural to hope for length of days, but who can say, he *will* live till to-morrow; or that he shall certainly be more virtuous twenty years hence, than he is to-day? Time often brings with it more guilt, and more sorrow; and he who trusts that he shall live to be old, for the purpose of regulating his passions, considers not that old age hath passions peculiar to itself. Nor is it less evident, that we are grossly presumptuous, if we defer our task, in expectation of long life: He that trusts his whole fortune on a bottom which hath wreck'd so many millions, and to which no man could ever safely trust, must be devoid of understanding: He runs his vessel on a rock in hopes of being saved on a plank.

I have given thee many hints concerning death: I hope some of them at least will be of use to thee. I have often enquired how my friends and acquaintances went off the stage: not how much they died worth, which is the usual question, but what sentiments they appeared to have in their dying hour.

JONATHAN, whom thou rememberest, was an abandoned, profligate wretch, and cared not in whose

debt

debt he ran, nor what diffention he lighted up, provided he could fatisfy his wants, and gratify his appetites and his pride. He had not a filver tongue, yet he had fo much wit and cunning, in the art of making people believe he was in earneft; and fo much refolution in the execution of his projects; and fuch fkill in evading law, that he laughed at all the juftices of the peace in the county. The wickednefs of his mind fhewed itfelf in a thoufand evil deeds: when he died, he did not feem fenfible that he muft give any account.———O miferable condition!

Not fo was RICHARD, though he had been guilty of many irregularities, and could not fatisfy his confcience on many accounts. I one day afked him, why he was fo fad? I fhall never forget his anfwer; he faid, "The foul, my friend, is a moft ferious "thing, and it muft either be fad here for a mo- "ment, or be fad for ever!" I have reafon to believe he died a penitent.

PETER was another of my acquaintance: he was a clever fellow, and fit for all manner of work; he had lively parts, and was active and laborious in whatever he undertook: his great blemifhes were inconftancy, difregard to truth, and the modern carelefs way of living. I faw him on his death bed, and heard him fay, "*Good God, what have I been* "*about, and where am I going!*" From whence I hoped he was not devoid of fentiments of contrition.

It was much the fame with ESQ. WILLIAM: indeed he difcourfed with a reverend gentleman concerning the immortality of the foul, and man's eternal ſtate; and weeping ſaid, "*O my poor ſoul, whither wilt thou go!*" When his father came to viſit him he ſaid, "*O ſir, your kindneſs hath undone me; I abuſed the ample ſupply you gave me. Were I to live my time again, I would feed on bread and water, rather than pamper my paſſions to hurry me into ſuch monſtrous exceſſes.*"

Another gentleman in this neighbourhood, who had been employed in many great offices for a number of years, in his laſt moments ſaid, "*After ſo many years experience in buſineſs, noiſe, and ſplendor, I think the greateſt wiſdom is ſeriouſneſs; the beſt phyſic, temperance; and the beſt eſtate, a good conſcience;*" declaring that were he to live again, the time he had ſpent in the world, he would exchange the court for retirement; and the palace, for an hour's enjoyment of God in the chapel; adding theſe words, "*Now all things forſake me, except my God, my duty, and my prayer.*"

I believe thou doſt not remember NICHOLAS; he was a man who had maintained ſome character in the world; but was much addicted to pleaſure, and ſenſual gratifications, forbidden by the law of Chriſt. He did not underſtand much of any ſuch law, for he ſeldom went to church; and then it ſeemed to be rather to find fault, than in the ſpirit of humility, to receive inſtruction. He hardly ever looked into the New Teſtament; and I do not remember to have heard that he ever went to the ſacrament of the Lord's Supper. Upon the whole,

it

it can with no propriety be said, that he was a *wise man:* nor did it appear when he died, that he had any faith in Christ, and consequently he was not a *christian.* Indeed he seemed much confused in thought, and said, like my other acquaintance, whom I have mentioned, *Good God, where am I going!* From whence you may judge that he believed in a God, and the immortality of the soul, though he seemed to have no solid foundation whereon to build his hopes, or dispel his fears. This must be ever the case with those who live in the contempt, or neglect of the holy scriptures, the commandments of Christ, and the memorial which our Saviour has appointed as a remembrance of himself.

I understood from SIR RALPH's butler, a few months before his master died, that he desired the reverend minister, to make extracts out of the sacred writings, on the plainest, and most exact way, of making his peace with God; observing, with a sigh, "*how few men consider to what end they are born* *into the world, till they are near the time of leaving* *it.*" SIR RALPH had many virtues, but thou seest how miserably poor he was, with all his wealth; and how ignorant, with all his learning.

His intimate friend, the generous SIR GEORGE, with his last breath, spoke to his friends these memorable words, "*Alas! my friends, the best bequest which I can make to you, is to entreat, that you will govern your wills and affections by the will and word of God. I have lived, in what is called the highest part of life, yet in me you behold the end of this world,* and all its vanities. *I repent of all my life, but that part of it which I spent in communing with God, and doing good!"*

The other day, when I went to see my acquaintance PHILIP, thinking him on his death bed, I asked him, *if he thought of God?* I am shocked when I recollect his answer; he said, " *O it is not come to that yet.*" Still he flattered himself with a continuance in life; and being so much estranged from religion, he fondly imagined, one *Lord have mercy on me!* when his breath was departing from him would be sufficient: and yet this man had been often advised by our worthy curate, to amend his wicked and careless life, and read the scriptures, and receive the sacrament.

When Mr. ABRAHAM enquired of the minister, how he should proceed to make his peace with God, he gave this advice; " *Read the New Testament; there you will find the words of eternal life; this book hath God for its author, salvation for its end, and truth without any mixture of error for its matter.*" Thrice happy are those who read that book with care, and learn that divine charity, which covereth the multitude of human infirmities.

My cousin THOMAS, long before his death, often told me his opinion, that charity in its full meaning, and rightly understood, contains all christian graces; he said, " those who have not this divine principle have no good in them." His piety kept pace with his charity: I believe he died the death of the righteous!

teous! These last are striking proofs of the advantages of virtue.

People of our condition differ not much: they have oftentimes less sensibility; and as they live, so they die. Let us strive to live well, as there is no possibility of dying well without a good life.

DISCOURSE XV.

The comparative characters of men and women, as displayed in their last hours. Deaths and behaviours of some distinguished persons, particularly Amelia and Eleanor. Duty of comforting and exhorting our friends on their death-bed.

IN regard to women, I cannot tell thee so much of them as of my own sex, and perhaps there is not so much to tell, of their difference of characters, and difference of behaviour in their last hours. The lives of women, are comparatively most free from atrocious guilt; from a habit of obedience, they live most submissively to the decrees of heaven: perhaps, being less deeply engaged in views of avarice and ambition, their chief guilt may consist in *envy* and *vanity*; vices, which in every station of life they are apt to overlook, or not discover. Envy, because beauty is so much their object; and vanity, from levity and desire of distinction in dress. Every one should be contented with her person, and the most fit apparel for her condition.

My cousin LUCY fell a sacrifice to vanity. She was one among the many thousands who have some virtues blended with many faults; she could not properly be called vicious, but she was very far from being virtuous. In short she did not act as if she remembered her end, and therefore could hardly avoid doing amiss. She seemed to delight only in mirth and festivity, music, dancing, public shows, &c. Thus instead of improving her understanding, correcting her will, and becoming the more attentive to admonition, and learning to be humble, devout, and useful, she acquired the reputation of a *giddy girl*. In the same degree that she neglected these duties, they became tasteless and insipid, and she had no heart for them. Having forgotten wherein her highest excellency consisted, she could not look backward with any true satisfaction, nor forward with any joyful confidence: but she thought very little of any thing, except the amusements of the present moment; and ever appeared to be disturbed. Death at length surprized her; and *surprized* we all must be, if we do not live as if the present day might be our last. She went through the common ceremonies of physicians, nurses, and friends, with as much decency as generally attends a death-bed, where the chief concern is to administer medicines to the body. God forbid that I should sit in judgment on her soul; but neither could I ever find any solid foundation whereon to rest my hopes. She seemed to die as she had lived, in a state of insensibility.

My master, I remember, made a remark, that the Mahometans generally die with the name of God in their mouths; that is, as long as they can speak, they repeat the word *Allah!* as if in this invocation, the dependance of poor mortals on the verge of eternity, the terrors of the soul were calmed, or her hopes exalted.

He also spoke of the solemnity in Portugal of putting malefactors to death at the place of execution: they constantly repeated, O Jesus! Jesus! *till they were hanging by the neck.*

It is always recommended to us to think on the mercies of God, to pray to him, to receive the sacrament of our Lord's Supper, as our last spiritual nourishment, to have a minister to pray by us, and to hear our friends read pious books. Among the number of books, I know of none more solid or more comfortable, than *Sherlock on death*.

Concerning a calm resignation, accompanied by generosity, my master was pleased with the story of a *French lady*. Happening to be bled by a surgeon, who had entertained a secret passion for her, the condition of the lady being much superior to his, upon uncovering her arm, he was visibly confused: This was observed; however, with great affability she desired him to go on in his work: and he cut an artery, instead of opening a vein. He immediately discovered his mistake, and the lady was as soon sensible, that she must die in consequence of it: but far from loading him with bitter reproaches, she saw with compassion the anguish of the unhappy man,

man, and submitted to providence. She went still farther; for thinking this event would injure his reputation as a surgeon, she made a handsome provision for him in her will; and died with that greatness of mind, which a good understanding, supported by the noble sentiments of christian piety and generosity, inspires! Was not this great? Dost think thou should'st have done the same, under the like circumstances?

With all their imperfections, women are called the *devout sex*; and I have already remarked to thee, that there is nothing great and noble, even in martyrdom, wherein women have not been, in all ages, distinguished. Mrs. ASKEW, among many others, a single gentle-woman, aged 25, was cruelly persecuted, and at last suffered martyrdom; being burnt in Smithfield, in the reign of Henry VIII. She died praying for her murderers.

Why, my dear child, in thy humble state, should'st not thou be as ready to die, for the glory of God, and the welfare of thine own soul, as the greatest of the children of men? But very few, in these days, are put to any severe trial. Never shall I forget the manner of thy dear mother's death. She seemed perfectly reconciled, as if she were happily arrived at her journey's end, after travelling through the rough ways of penury, and weathering the storms of affliction. The truth is, she had lived an honest and a religious life; her mind was in peace; she was full of the hopes of the reward of the righteous, and she looked up to the *finisher of her faith*, even

Christ

Christ her Redeemer! She had constantly and steadfastly fixed her eye on a judgment to come; and this furnished her with such principles of action, as can be learnt no other way. She had thought of death familiarly, and therefore she did not *fear* it. Indeed, she was so truly pious, and full of hope, that to my imagination, in those early days, she appeared to ascend the clouds in triumph! O my child, may thy death, whenever it comes, be like her's; I think thou wilt then most assuredly die the death of the righteous!—Why do I wander back so many years, and set my wounds a bleeding!—Thou art her image! May thy virtues be like her's, that thou mayest at length shine as the stars of heaven!

Thou rememberest AMELIA. She was a young woman of the most excellent disposition! Her modesty could be equalled by nothing but the gracefulness of her smiles, and the benignity of her temper. Her dutifulness to her parents, and their judicious care and tenderness, were become famous. She was never seen to be at a loss for employment, nor out of humour for any cross accident. Her own passions being always calm, she was a guide and monitor to all her acquaintance. Unpractised in any art of falshood or cunning, flattery or insinuation, by the resistless power of her discourse she commanded the affections of all her acquaintance. She sung most sweetly; but she was never tempted to wakes, or fairs, or to keep any company but such as her parents recommended. Her winning softness was attended with a turn of mind, as serious as uncommon,

common, and out of fashion. The sentiments she had committed to writing, which were found after her death, abundantly proved, how justly she thought of her own dissolution, and how much her heart was devoted to her maker. And as if heaven had marked her for its own, ere she had well seen twenty years, having filled up the measure of her virtue, she was called to the society of her kindred angels. O what a loss was sustained in her!— Glad should I be, to speak so well of any man of my acquaintance, who, having died so young, was possessed of so much intrinsic worth!

Thou hast lately seen a fresh instance how precarious life is, and how it ought to be spent; I hope thou wilt remember it with thy expiring breath. 'Tis but the other day, thy much loved friend, and the companion of thy earliest days, AMELIA's cousin, the sweet ELEANOR, took her flight also. Hardly to complete eighteen years, is young: though half who are born, are dead by seventeen years; so many drop in infancy and childhood *.

We cannot say this young woman lived not half her days; for she filled up the time that heaven had appointed for her. Her course of virtue was early run; and the great arbiter of life and death, was pleased to call her to rest!

Travellers seldom complain that they come too soon to their journey's end; and this young woman, who died well, had surely lived long enough for

* Of 1000 born, 498 are dead by the age of 15; that is, in great cities.

herself;

herself; and as for the world in general, we must leave it in the hands of God.

In the very blossom of ELEANOR's life, her virtues were fragrant! She was early at her duty, and as active as a bee; and the produce of her labour, as sweet as honey: she was no less a mistress of her needle, than of what belonged to the dairy; and industry was her pleasure and delight. In love for her brothers and sisters, no body excelled her. She was affable to every one, and always ready to plead the cause of pity, and of peace: no one could be a truer advocate for misery and distress. When she had nothing else to give, her tears stood in her eyes; but she comforted herself by thinking, that there is no affliction for which religion has not provided a remedy. She spoke of those whom she could not praise, with a tenderness that expressed her universal benevolence. She went to church twice every sabbath-day, and read the Bible and Testament, with such attention, as to understand what was necessary to her happiness in both worlds. At her leisure she read other good books; and carefully avoided those dangerous stories which corrupt the heart, and pollute the fancy.—Guarded against the extremes of melancholy and carelessness, she possessed her soul in that happy chearfulness and composure, which are the ordinary companions of innocence; and the best instructors how to die!—In the gifts of nature, she was no less happy; being in temper sweet, in manners gentle, in conversation pleasing, and in voice melodious.—Humility, and the love of truth,

truth, prevented her being given to affectation, for she had too much sense to be proud. With her sweetness of disposition, she had a large portion of courage, which she wisely thought necessary to the conduct of life; well knowing, that nothing can embitter life so much as fear; nor any thing be more fantastic, than false delicacy; as if women were not to be taught to die. She was sensible that nothing can conquer this unmanly passion, which is apt to shew itself in such various forms, but religion and the exercise of reason. With what glorious strength of mind and resignation, she spoke of her own death; shewing forth her confidence in the mercy of God, through Christ, the Redeemer of the world! The same sentiments, and tranquility of spirit, which rendered her life so amiable, attended her expiring breath. Thou knowest the manner of her death was truly desirable, and her life a glorious object for imitation.

Dost thou weep, my child, at this detail? Soft sorrows rather heal than wound the spirit; there is no bitterness in such grief. Thy tears bespeak thy tenderness; but there are many reasons why thou should'st wipe them, and be comforted. She hath happily escaped the dangers with which this life abounds. Calm and serene, she possessed the most peaceful purity, and unmixed hope; and exchanged this world for one much better. The truth is, that providence is so wonderfully kind to us, that in age we are grown ripe for death, and in youth there seems to be more courage, or less

reluct-

reluctance, from the mind being lefs corrupt, and from having fewer attachments to the world. In both cafes we may fay with the poet; We are

"Taught half by reafon, half by mere decay,
"To welcome death, and calmly pafs away."

Is it not a plentiful fource of confolation, to think of being out of the reach of affliction, and what is more, beyond the poffibility of offending God! Thou, my child, knoweft not the dangerous fmiles of a treacherous world. Comfort thyfelf! "*Tears* will not water the lovely plant to make it "grow again.—*Sighs* will not give her new breath; "nor canft thou furnifh her with life and fpirits, by "the wafte of thine own." Complain not of the fhortnefs of thy joy; nor let thy lofs in her, turn to thy difadvantage. Be thankful to thy maker, that thou enjoyedft it fo long; and in thy forrow, forget not to pray, "*Thy will, O God, be done!*" "To her, "virtue was grey hairs, and an unfpotted life, old "age." Let the remembrance of her good qualities live in thine heart; and in proportion to thy love for her, let her ftill be thy friend and monitor. Think of her happinefs; and in that reflection, be happy thyfelf.—Wipe thy tears: and whilft thou offereft up thy pious lamentation, let this inftance of her well fpent life, teach thee what is the defign of God, in giving breath to mortals; and rather mourn for thofe who are *living in fin*, than for thy friend who died in the practice of virtue. Bring the perfuasion, that death cannot be very diftant, fo far into practice as to be always attentive to thy thoughts, words and deeds. If thou vieweft death in a true light, not merely as the finifher of life, but as the introducer into a ftate which is to laft for ever, it will rouze every faculty of thy foul, and call up all thy attention. And fince there is in nature, fo great a repugnance to the thought of death, let it operate as the ftrongeft reafon " for cleanfing thyfelf *from* all filthinefs of the flefh and fpirit, perfecting holinefs in the fear of God." This is a confideration for the wifeft and beft of mankind, at all ages; that were it only to die in comfort, the labour of living virtuoufly would be abundantly repaid. I call it labour, only as labour is pleafure; for no pleafure exceeds that of thinking and acting right, and doing good: Nor can any comfort exceed that of keeping a glorious profpect of eternal happinefs in view.

In ficknefs, or advanced years, people continually deceive themfelves as to the approach of death; and provided they live well, this only proves the kindnefs of the great Lord of life. Two of my acquaintance, lately dead, were both far gone in a confumption, and deemed incurable: each faid he thought the other would die very foon, but neither feemed to imagine his own death near. Wife men correct their own faults, by obferving wherein others are defective. With us, things go very much by fafhion; and it is not our cuftom to fpeak of the approach of death, or the ftate of the mind of our

friend

friend or relation, not even in the moſt gentle terms. This is one reaſon why ſo few think about it. Inſtead of giving the moſt aſſiſtance that is practicable, to thoſe who ſtand moſt in need, we give the leaſt that can be imagined.

Were people of ability to talk the language of reaſon and religion upon theſe awful occaſions, it would probably operate on many a ſick perſon, and make the approach of death leſs dreadful. The chriſtian faith requires of us to rejoice *always*, and conſequently to look on life and death indifferently, but as they adminiſter to the honour of God, and the welfare of mankind. Confidence in God, robs death of his terrors:—We only drop aſleep.

If near relations were to endeavour, by *reading*, *prayer*, or *diſcourſe*, to inſpire the *dying* perſon with courage to bear pain and death, the living might learn the better *how to die*. The approach of death, like other dangers, is apt to terrify the fearful. This being the laſt ſcene, it ſeems ſtrange that the deareſt friends ſhould be ſo paſſive, and do nothing towards brightening the hopes of a bliſsful immortality! We ſuppoſe that it will anſwer no good purpoſe, to ſpeak of death to one on a ſick bed, unleſs the patient is a moſt abandoned wicked perſon; and yet to ſuch it may be of the leaſt uſe, of which I told thee of ſome inſtances. Our indifference in this article, is ſtamped with ſuch a mark of faſhionable authority, that any conduct contrary to it, would be ſuſpected of enthuſiaſm or hypocriſy.

As

As a proof of this, the ministers of God's word are not always required to attend, though good men, on such occasions, appear as angels of comfort. This is wonderful, but I fear it is too true; and amongst other things, makes the folly more apparent in those who trust they shall repent, though they know not *when*, nor *where*, nor *how*. They are sure they shall die, some time or other, and they observe that people usually die in beds; and conclude they shall have a chance of a *death-bed repentance*. O my child, live prepared for death, and in a concern of such vast moment, trust not to thou knowest not what.

Remember, if thou puttest off 'till to-morrow, that which thou could'st do to day, wert thou about to die, thou wilt not only be guilty of presumption, but it is highly probable thou wilt never do it. I will tell thee, my child, why I think so.—*To-morrow*, and *to-morrow*, creep on, in a stealing pace, to the end of our days. *To-morrow* can never be *to-day*. We never can be sure of thinking to-morrow as we think to-day; but of this we are sure, that the lamp of life burns out, though behind the curtain; and that when the oil is spent, darkness must follow.

The general consideration of death, shews the folly of immoderate grief, as well as excessive joy, for any thing that befals us. It likewise shews the madness of the daring sinner, who mocks at the fear of God! His last day draws near, when he will stand trembling with terror before his tremendous judge

judge! The approaching day of the good is also coming on, in the same pace; but this will be to them a day of triumph, beyond the power of language to describe! " The sorrows of the poor and " the despised, will then fly away like the shades of " night at the approach of the sun." This is matter for constant chearfulness; it is more: it is joy and delight. That such glory may be thine, shall be my constant prayer!

DISCOURSE XVI.

Reflections on the certainty of death, and the resurrection. The New Testament our only true guide. The character of our Saviour described in it.

HAST thou thought seriously of the subject of our yesterday's conversation. I hope it will live in thy memory, as long as it shall please heaven to give thee breath. Thou feest how sincerely I wish to promote thy well-being, not here only, but also beyond the grave: I would gladly do the same to all the children of men; and thus partake of all the good they may receive here, and arrive at the possession of in that country where all distinctions cease, but those of virtue and vice.

I told thee thy chance of life for fifteen years, and my own for five: yet hast not thou often heard people say, when they approach to sixty, " *three-score years! that is no age!*" They know perhaps,

that

that in a *thousand* born, a few remain alive at fourscore *; and yet the chance is, that half the people of 60 will be dead before 70 †.

Alas! poor ten years to strut in, about the world! And do they consider that these ten years are but broken fragments of time, divided out amongst the number of candidates for life: some have only *one* or *two*, and others *eight* or *nine*; and, one with another, they hardly obtain above five or six years of the ten. Many are so unwilling to die, they secretly envy ignorance, poverty, or pain, where they think there is a prospect of length of days.

* Of 72 persons (the remainder of 1000 born) being 70 years of age, by the course of mortality 55 of them die within ten years; and consequently only 27 of the 1000 remain alive at the age of 80.

† Of 135 (the remainder of 1000 born) being 60 years of age, before ten years are expired, 63 of them die, which is not far short of the half part, to die before any one reaches to 70 years.

I think it is the celebrated physician, Dr. Cadogan, who says that the life of man is not properly seventy years, but ninety; which he divides, 30 to go up, 30 to stand, and 30 to go down; and I believe he may be near the mark, supposing men to live in the best climates of the earth, and that all their passions and appetites were regulated by reason and christian faith; but taking things as they are, with all the heats and colds, and dry and moist, passions not half controlled, and appetites so much indulged for momentary gratifications, we must agree with the pious psalmist, and fix it at 70 years, with this exception, that about 27 in 1000 born, live to 80: for no creature has such resources to repair his animal frame, as man: reason being so evidently given him for his own preservation. At the same time his frame is of so wonderful a texture, that not only the parts wear as they are used, and according to their original strength, as derived from the parent; but it is so small a part of mankind as 27 in 1000 born, who live to fourscore: and these suffer decrepidness, disease, and pain: many who have been accustomed to excess, lose also the powers of the mind.

Were

Were it duly attended to, nothing could exalt us so much as the consideration of a life to come; nothing is so noble, extensive, and delightful, in contemplation! It is what is aimed at in all the distinctions of man and brute, all learning in high life, and all knowledge in an humble condition verge to the same point: All the glory of this world is as nothing to it. And indeed mortality appears so continually at our doors and windows, in our chambers, and fields, that one would imagine we should avail ourselves of the promises of the gospel as our only relief; and as the only effectual preservation of a rational life; but when we do not learn such lessons in our youth, we hardly ever come to a right understanding of them: yet learn them we must at some time or other, or retire unprepared to give up our account. If thou, my child, wilt try the experiment, and make the next life the first object of thy thoughts, take my word for it, thou wilt, as thou advancest, enjoy a glorious and delightful entertainment, which common mortals are strangers to. To perform all our social duties with joy here on earth, and to receive a still higher joy in hope in a life to come, must give charms to every object, and take out the sting of misery; proving the wonderful goodness of heaven in making every thing happen for good to the *good*.

Thus to be good is to be happy in the truest sense; and so far as we mortals can reach the true standard of goodness, we approach the felicity of angels, whatever our condition may be, as providence may
have

have cast our lot. I am afraid this is a secret to a great part of mankind, though it be evidently the leading principle of the gospel, and most intimately connected with our progress in holiness. It is impossible to *live*, and *not to die*; and God hath made it impossible to die, without being happy, or miserable after death.

We hear of each others bodily complaints, 'till we grow sick of the subject; but when didst thou hear any one talk *properly* of the joys he hoped for after death? Yet if our practice kept pace with our christian profession, we might animate each other in this glorious pursuit.

" The wise look forward into futurity, and con-
" sider what will be their condition, millions of
" ages hence, as well as what it is at present!"
And how can the true spirit of christianity be revived, unless we meditate on the happy immortality which it promises?

Such being the defects in the practice and intercourse of nominal christians, I know not what better advice I can give thee, than to converse with thine own heart; to read; to think; to regulate thy thoughts, and observe the tendency of thy actions; calling thyself to account in a reasonable manner every day.

The *less* thou examinest thy *heart*, the *more* deceitful it will become; and the more it will flatter. Yet when thou dost examine it, be not *disheartened* at thine own imperfections. Every thing may be reformed by grace, and improved by care. Compassion paffion is due to ourfelves. A feverity of *felf-chaftifement*, beyond the bounds which reafon warrants, and our truft in God demands, leads to melancholy, or defpair. Aufterities, beyond certain bounds, have not the marks of true religion: To be truly *wife*, we muft be in good fpirits, chearful and good-humoured: piety itfelf implies an agreeable and pleafing quality. In many cafes we ought to *remember* our *own* faults, and *forget thofe of others*; yet, though confcious of our imperfections, we fhould take pains to confider ourfelves in *that light*, wherein it is moft probable we fhall benefit; drawing this conclufion, that *diftruft* of God, is of all evils the greateft, excepting *defpair*.

Endeavour, my child, to conquer the world, and the vanities thereof, or thefe will conquer thee: It is neceffary to contend for *victory*, in humble confidence that when thou haft done thy endeavour; though thine own merit cannot fave thee, yet wilt thou be accepted. The language of fcripture is, " Be thou faithful unto death, and I will give thee a crown of life."

Remember the counfel and admonition of our great Lord and mafter, when he bid his difciples, and confequently all his followers through all generations, to be of *good cheer*, for that *he* had *overcome* the world. If thou wilt walk in his fteps, thou wilt find he has overcome it for *thee*. Be affured that whenever the thoughts of immortality are habitually rejected, thou art either living in a finful habit, in defiance of heaven, or thou doft not believe the pro-

G mifes

mifes of Chrift, fo as to look forward towards them with a grateful, a joyful, and a courageous heart.

The great doctrine of the refurrection, is properly an object of *faith*; but now that it is fully revealed to us, nothing is more agreeable to *reafon*; and the *works* of God give evidence to it. I know, that the corn which I fow, corrupts, and lies dead in the earth, but it brings forth its feed in abundance in due feafon. This is the *work* of God, and we fee the effects with our eyes; but how they are produced we know not. Thou feeft them, and believeft in them; is it not highly reafonable to believe in God's *word* alfo? We have the moft undoubted evidence, that Chrift *arofe* from the dead, and that he *raifed* the dead. The miracles he did, gave proof of the will of the Almighty, as well as of his power; and we have the exprefs promife of Chrift, if we are really his difciples, that where he is, there we fhall be alfo. St. *John* x. xiv. chap.

If thou therefore meaneft to deferve the glorious name of a *chriftian*, be zealous for thy great mafter's honour! Examine into the circumftances of his life, with care and attention; and fhew thy love for him by thy obedience to his precepts: all other inftructions compared to them are light in the balance. Thou wilt find them in the New Teftament, moft clearly marked out*. As:

* Inftances of the life of our Saviour propofed to imitation, from Burkit's expofition of the New Teftament, at the clofe of his remarks on St. John's Gofpel, where thofe who are poffeffed of this ufeful book, may find proper comments on thefe inftances of our Saviour's life.

1. His

1. His early piety. *Luke* xi. 46, 47.
2. —obedience to his earthly parents. *Luke* ii. 51.
3. —unwearied diligence in doing good. *Acts* x. 38.
4. —humility and lowliness of mind. *Mat.* xi. 29.
5. The unblameableness and inoffensiveness of his life and actions. *Mat.* xix. 27.
6. His eminent self-denial. *Phil.* ii. 7, 8.
7. —contentment in a low and mean condition in this world. *Luke* ix. 58.—*Phil.* iv. 11.
8. —frequent performance of the duty of private prayer. *Luke* vi. 12.—*Mark* i. 35.
9. —affectionate performance of the duty of praise and thanksgiving. *Mat.* xi. 25.—*John* xi. 41.
10. —compassion towards those who were miserable, and in distress. *Mat.* xx. 34.
11. —spiritual, entertaining, and useful discourse. *Luke* xiv. 7. xxiv. 13.
12. His free, familiar, sociable behaviour. *Mat.* xi. 19.—*Luke* v. 29.
13. —patience under sufferings and reproaches. 1 *Peter* ii. 21, 22.
14. —readiness to forgive injuries. *Luke* xxiii. 34.
15. —laying to heart the sins as well as sufferings of others. *Mark* iii. 5.
16. —zeal for the public worship of God. *John* ii. 17.
17. —glorifying his father in all he did. *John* xvii. 4.
18. —impartiality in reproving sin. *Mat.* xxii. 23.
19. —universal obedience to his father's will, and chearful submission to his father's pleasure. *Mat.* xxvi. 20.

20.—laws and practice of universal holiness, both in heart and life. *Luke* iv. 34.

Keep thine eye on this model in every action of thy life; it will give thee more comfort and joy in the end, than volumes of other reading, or all the pleasures the earth can furnish.

What is the *world*? What hath been the fate even of whole nations? Where are the antient people, the *Jews*, who made so great a figure in their time, as the sacred history informs us? What variety of national punishments did their sins occasion, 'till they were at length cut off from the earth, as a people!—Where are the mighty empires of the Assyrians, the Babylonians, the Egyptians!—Where are the Romans, who were masters of the Jews, as the scriptures acquaint us, when under their ruler PONTIUS PILATE, the Lord of life was put to death upon the cross!—Those mighty states are wiped off the face of the earth! And what will be the fate of the earth itself, and all the glorious luminaries that surround it? The stars will fade away, and the sun be extinguished, at the command of the Most High. But still, my child, thou, who art as a worm, will live for ever! O glorious thought! worthy of a monarch's breast, and given by the hand of heaven to the meanest subject. If therefore at any time great misery should be thy lot, though *great misery* is seldom the lot of the virtuous, still consider that it will not last long: It will soon cease; or it will make an end of thee by death; and death will crown thy constancy with everlasting happiness!

DIS-

DISCOURSE XVII.

On superstition. Folly of believing in witches. Story of Dame Tempest. On enthusiasm. On melancholy.

IN contemplating the life of our Saviour, and the rules of behaviour which he hath taught, thou wilt find such hope and joy spring up in thy breast, as will banish all false apprehensions. Whatever thy lot may be, this will prevent thy falling into the blindness of *superstition*, the frenzy of *enthusiasm*, or the deplorable sighs of *melancholy*. There are many who pretend to genuine christianity, and yet have foisted into their religion, a vast variety of follies and iniquities. It is necessary on this occasion to warn thee against them.

Some *Papists* have carried superstition to the height of *idolatry*; insomuch that they even pray to deceased mortals, and kneel before images made of wood and stone. They pray to saints of their own making, as mediators for them with God; though it is so often, and so strongly declared in the scriptures, that *Christ* is our *only Mediator* and *Intercessor* at the throne of the Almighty. I have heard my master say, that he has seen, in popish countries, images carried about the streets, to which the people fell down upon their knees and prayed, ascribing to them the power of working miracles! Strange folly,

folly and credulity, which once stained the annals of our illustrious forefathers in this happy isle. To such heights of dotage and childishness may mankind be brought, when they have once deviated from the true worship of the one supreme and invisible God! Canst thou think there are any, in this land, so blind as to entertain this absurd faith? There *are* some, even at this time, when Papists themselves, in several popish countries, are every day discovering their errors and delusions. To such a height may false fear, and fantastic hope be carried, as to make people believe, that such a male, or female saint, can do such and such things for them: or if they make application with liberal presents, at the church or chapel dedicated to such a saint, he will avert evils, and give them success. These people also make vows and promises, as if God were to be bribed by their gifts and deeds of ostentatious charity. Their follies seem to be drawing to an end. What time the wisdom of God has fixed, he only knows.

Learn from hence what evils mankind are exposed to; and how happy we are, in being born in a land where the scriptures are in every one's hand, remembering that the greater our opportunities of obedience, the greater will be our condemnation if we do not avail ourselves of them, and that it may be more tolerable for *Tyre* and *Sidon* at the last judgment, than for us. See St. *Luke* x. 14.

Perhaps thou art not aware, that even good dispositions, if carried beyond their due bounds, and

not

not regulated by reason, may degenerate into vices. It is the fear of God, when unworthy notions are entertained of him, which produces superstition. In some countries this weakness has been considered as a crime, but I think it is rather an object of our compassion than of our anger. Some, to this day, make every thing to be *ominous*, and in their foolish opinion the most simple accidents threaten great evils: witness the croaking of a raven, or the ticking of a spider, or other insect vulgarly called a *deathwatch*. Thou hast seen some of our good neighbours, much disturbed at the oversetting a salt on the table; and by laying knives across; and if there happen to be just thirteen in number, in a company, they make it a reason for believing one of them will die within the course of the year; and not knowing who it will be, they all imagine what they please, and take pains to torment themselves. There are a thousand foolish whims, which are the true growth of superstition. It is hard to say, whether there be most folly, or madness in it; but it certainly argues a distrust of the wisdom and goodness of God: for how can we suppose that the all-wise ruler of the world, will discover any of his designs to man, by means so trifling and insignificant; or torment them by doubts and anxieties, founded on such circumstances?

Superstition prepares the mind to receive any impressions from artful persons, such as pretend to tell fortunes; and others yet more wicked, who deluding by false doctrines, and representing falsehood as truth,

truth, and vice as virtue, lead the unwary into great mischief, and sometimes into destruction. Thus superstition roots up the foundations of religion; and in no instance has it been productive of more tragical effects than in the belief of witchcraft. Be assured, that witches are nothing but the children of a sick brain. To imagine that the Lord of nature should impower the Prince of darkness to make a poor old woman an instrument, " to untie the winds, to swallow up ships in the waves, to blight the bladed corn, and to afflict a favourite child with fits or infanity," merely because she has been refused a trifle, when begging at the door, is altogether weak and absurd.

Our poor old neighbour *Dame Tempest*, has been called a witch, merely because the variety of her wretchedness has made her a miserable object. Her eyes are covered with a dreadful salt, and burning rheum—she trembles in speech—her hearing is much impaired—her garb is the emblem of poverty, composed of various colours, being patches with which industry and misery have loaden them. This poor creature has seen better days, but out-living all her children and her friends, and condemned to a solitary cottage, she hath appeared as an out-cast from the human race. She worked as long as she was able, but is now reduced to the miserable pittance of one shilling a week from the parish. Yet in the midst of all this accumulated distress, she possesses herself with patience and fortitude, looking forward to her dissolution with tranquility and hope.

When

When I visit her, she speaks to me with freedom and good sense. "You are as an angel sent from heaven, to help me to die in peace. They think me very miserable, but I am not so much so as I appear, were it only that I am contented to die! Death is to me most desirable: It is the inevitable lot of all, and consequently my privilege: If I suffer something to obtain it, the evil can be but of short duration."

Yet with all this christianity about her, so weak does credulity make mankind, that she is suspected of being what they call a witch—that is, a person in league with the devil!

When fear of evil is founded in a sense of guilt, repentance and amendment of life only can subdue it, and convert it into the genuine fear of God. There is but one way of fortifying thy soul against superstitious fear, and that is, by endeavouring with singleness of heart, to secure to thyself the friendship and protection of that Being, who disposes of all events, past, present, and to come; insomuch, that not a hair can fall from thy head but he knoweth it.

I must give thee another charge with regard to false notions of religion. I have heard people talk of *enthusiasts* who have totally neglected their families, their own health, and the concerns of this world, supposing this to be necessary to maintain an intercourse with the next. What a strange absurdity! In popish countries numbers of both sexes live on the spoils of the poor, and do nothing: but religion is so far from supposing, that we have not bodies to provide for, that there is hardly a leſſon in it, which does not teach ſomething that regards the good of the body, and whoever neglects his family, or his own health, from a miſtaken notion that he ſhall become more acceptable to God, will find that he is grievouſly miſtaken; for this is voluntarily to abandon himſelf, and be rendered incapable of many of thoſe duties, which the goſpel requires. " I was hungry and ye gave me food; " I was naked and ye clothed me; I was ſick and " ye viſited me." Theſe, our great friend, the Redeemer of the world, informs us, are works which he will regard as done to himſelf, if we do them to others who are in need. And though they muſt flow from a good ſpirit, they ſurely relate to the body. That there are enthuſiaſts of this untoward and ridiculous turn of mind, I do indeed believe; but I am perſuaded their number is very inconſiderable; and that theſe ought rather to be ranked as madmen than merely as enthuſiaſts.

Though I give thee this caution againſt a falſe notion which pious people ſometimes fall into, I believe there are very few inſtances in this proteſtant land, wherein induſtry is checked by piety, ſo as to neglect a proviſion for the body. The ſobriety recommended by religion, naturally tends to promote induſtry.

Another evil is *melancholy:* this ſees misfortunes which never come. It anticipates thoſe that will come: and it aggravates them when they are arrived. In effect, it runs to meet thoſe calamities
which

which we should rather fly from, or by opposing them with courage, conquer them. Superstition and melancholy are nearly related, and generally meet in the same person. Upon the whole, we have all need of a faithful friend, or a severe enemy to admonish and correct; or persuade us to our duty, or shew us our faults, so as to make us ashamed of them. Happy are those who have such a friend! Thou findest one in me whose fidelity thou mayest depend on. These evils are to be guarded against with the more care, as they often take the name of virtues, and few who are infected by them are sensible of their disease: being the effect of gross folly or weakness of mind, the same weakness renders the remedy hard to come at.

DISCOURSE XVIII.

Charity for differences in opinion. The great importance of a good conscience.

WORSE than even superstition, enthusiasm, or melancholy, is *uncharitableness*. Every people and language have notions of things peculiar to themselves, but want of charity is the rock on which so many millions have run, when they have fondly imagined themselves to be in a fair course. The opinions of men are as different as their persons, and the rash manner in which we sometimes hear sentence pronounced on each other, is no proof of wisdom; but on the contrary, leads many into a labyrinth of uncharitable blindness.

I believe, my child, that all mankind who act agreeably to the dictates of their conscience, according to the lights afforded them, will be accepted by God: I believe this, because I hope the sincerity of my own heart will be accepted by him, though I should err: and for the same reason that I would shew mercy to others, I hope mercy will be shewn to me.

God forbid that thou shouldest look upon any one as a foe to heaven, merely because he differs from thee in opinion; or be an enemy to any person, who as far as thou knowest is a friend to God. Do not thou, who art dust and ashes, pretend to decide the fate of others; nor let it affect the benevolence of thy mind, though others should presumptuously sit in judgment upon thee. Adore thy Maker for his boundless goodness to all the children of men, whatever their situation may be. If thou hast a deep sense of such goodness, it will naturally inspire thy mind with the *tenderest charity*, and the *truest benevolence*, towards all thy fellow creatures, by whatever faith, mode of worship, or worldly interests they are distinguished. This is the way, my dear child, to follow the great Lord and teacher of the christian world!

If thou thinkest thy neighbour in an error, which it is not in thy power to correct, it is enough if thou avoidest falling into the same mistake. Still I say,

say, be *charitable*, and leave him to that being who is infinite in wisdom and mercy; and who will most assuredly adjust all those differences, which men so often, and so vainly attempt to regulate.

I have many times observed, that whether in religious, or worldly concerns, "what men say for themselves, and what their adversaries infer, or represent them as saying, are generally two very different things: and those who will not be at the pains to consider distinctly, what each side alledges for itself, but will judge of either, by the character or representation made of it, will be for ever led into erroneous judgments concerning men and things, and continue unavoidably ignorant of the true state of the matter in question." Experience has taught me that this is so much the case, I am always slow of believing the vulgar report.

As creatures of one common nature, endowed with such noble principles of action, and yet limited to so short a time, one might suppose that nothing but love and harmony would be found here on earth: unhappily, how often do we observe the contrary! Yet it is most apparent, that a benevolent mind is a feast of joy administered by the hands of angels; as a malignant disposition, is an engine of torture brought from the regions of the damned.

The *gay world*, whose pursuits do not allow them much time for enquiry, are too apt to reproach the most serious, be their faith and practice ever so pure; and frequently represent them as of some sect or other. The most ignorant are always the most conceited; and unable to discern their own folly, or the wisdom of others.

If therefore it should fall to thy lot to be reproached for thy piety, as if, being pious, therefore thou must have adopted some false tenet or opinion, bear it patiently: rather think it the misfortune of others in judging ill, than thine own in being ill-judged of: most of us have a greater propensity to detect small faults, than to applaud great virtues.

In general, mankind live more according to fashion and opinion, which are very changeable, than according to the rules of wisdom, which are steady and lasting; and as they live themselves, so they judge of others. This, alas! is too general a propensity.

Upon the whole, I hope thou wilt treat all foolish or unjust reproach with indifference; yet as occasions offer, it may be not only warrantable, but necessary, to defend thyself by explaining thy opinion, and recommending peace and good will. Contradiction, expressed in gross terms, inflames the *passions* of others; and passionate disputes hardly ever enlighten the understanding, though they often extinguish the light of reason. " In heat of argument " men are commonly like those that are tied back " to back; close joined, and yet they cannot see one " another." My master used to mention an excellent rule to be observed in disputes, " That we " should give *soft* words, and *hard* arguments, and " not strive to *vex*, but to *convince* our opponents."

" There

" There is as much wisdom in bearing with
" other people's *defects*, as in being sensible of their
" *good qualities*; and we should make the *follies* of
" others, a *warning* and *instruction* to ourselves."
This is the way to preserve the mind in charity and
peace, to *correct ourselves*, and to reform the world.

Thou, my dear child, art yet comparatively in a
state of innocence.—Mayest thou continue in it!—
and let me die in peace!—Remember, that " it is
" always term time in the court of conscience; and
" every one committing a trespass is a prisoner of
" *justice*, as soon as it is done," whether it be
known or not. What even thy *conscience* but whispers thee to be wrong, there is so strong a presumption will be displeasing to God, that thou should'st
forbear and fly from it, lest it sting thee to death;
for a wounded spirit who can bear?

There is no remaining fixt to one point; thou
wilt be always going on improving, or giving way
and growing worse. Time never stands still: our
nature subjects us to change; and our change should
always be for the better. Thus, though thou
shouldst remain low in condition, thou mayest rank
high in virtue; but all the wealth in the world will
not compensate for a *bad conscience*. Let a little
time pass, and all the distinctions about which mankind make such a bustle, and often hazard their
conscience and their souls, drop into the grave.
The earth will cover us all, ere long; and she herself will be changed; and therefore it is absurd to

be

be exalted or dejected, beyond measure, about any thing here below.

I will venture to assure thee, from the variety I have seen in my own life, that *reality* scarce ever equals *imagination.* Our earthly delights are seldom so sweet in enjoyment, as they are in expectation; but the pleasures of the understanding are always sweet in proportion as they arise from a quiet conscience, and a mind full of hope.

To be sensible when the conscience is wounded, is one part of its cure, provided we keep the sore open till it heals effectually; and not as those who skin it over, or do any thing to divert the pain. " It fareth with men of an evil conscience, when they must *die*, as it does with riotous spendthrifts, when they must pay their debts: they have declined coming to account, from a distrust of their inability to pay, till the hand of justice overtakes them." Think, O my child, that divine justice comes with *leaden* feet, yet if we persist in our offences, it will strike with *iron* hands. Be thy fortune good or be it ill, heaven, preserve thy soul unspotted from the world!

DISCOURSE XIX.

The advantages of humility. On a low station. A virtuous and vicious conduct contrasted. The fatal consequences of vice.

IN common life, we esteem humility, one of the most excellent of virtues: With respect to morals, as dependant on religion, it seems to be the consummation of all virtues: without it a *christian* actually loses his name. It makes us love our fellow-creatures, and often attracts their affection; but can excite no malice or envy. To be proud and humane implies a kind of contradiction. Humility has one peculiar advantage, adapted to all circumstances, for it sets us above the world in the truest and best sense; for " he that is little in his own eyes, will not be troubled to be thought so by others." The consequence of which is, freedom from temptations to pride and envy; whilst it bids fair to subdue anger, ambition, and all other turbulent passions, which are so apt to inflame and disturb the human breast. Thus, what is most pleasing to God, is at the same time most productive of worldly happiness. " Blessed are the *meek*, for they shall inherit the earth."

Thou hast promised me in the most solemn manner, to be humble; that is, to use thy endeavours to to be so. Our Saviour commands us to learn of him, for that he is meek and lowly; and if we follow his example, we shall find rest unto our souls. From whence we may easily conclude, that we shall not find any such rest, if we are turbulent, ambitious, covetous, or *discontented*. One sally of anger, one emotion of envy, or unchaste desire, naturally begets another; and till we conquer ourselves, we certainly shall not be at peace. The mind is the seat of empire in the little world within us, and if its subjects mean to be at peace, they must be quiet.

If any temptation creates an extraordinary tumult in thy breast, concerning what is right to be done, consult thy conscience, and humble thyself before thy God. In doing this thou mayest possibly feel some smart, but this is of the kind we are sensible of, on the dressing a wound by a salve which heals it. Humility hath amazing properties, and operates marvellously on the passions. If against thy better judgment, thy inclination pulls thee with the cords of iniquity, fly to thy prayers for succour. Think of the effects of ingratitude: consider the terrors of an *offended conscience*: bring that to thine eyes immediately, which must surely happen:—and startle at the bitter pangs of remorse!

We often hear the sober part of mankind talk of the necessity of warring against nature, but they mean this of the corruptions of our nature. To oppose the evil propensities to which we find ourselves inclined, is the best proof of being friends to religion. If our passions rebel, we must war against them,

them, and reduce them to obedience and reason: By whatever name thou callest thy inclinations, it is thy duty to oppose them. The task will become easy, as soon as thou art accustomed to it; the struggle will be crowned with victory: and the more early thou beginnest the easier the task will be. We are assured that the power of conquering will be given us, if we seek it with a sincere heart.

Take my advice; read the New Testament every day of thy life, though it should be but a verse or two, in order to supply thyself with some good thought. Devote thy mind to these oracles of God. Transcribe what thou readest into thine heart, and cherish it in thy bosom.

If the circumstances of the life and death of Christ, what he *did* and *suffered*, and what he hath *commanded* and *forbidden*, were made the rules of life, we should feel our existence in a very different manner; and our days would pass in peace. Such *lessons* are necessary *at all times*; but if we do not learn and relish them, whilst we are in youth, how are we to form our taste, and model our lives, as we advance in years? If we dwell on the sense contained in the scriptures, and consider them as the words of eternal life, we shall not be at a loss to find the road to a happy eternity. What years have I squandered! How often have I offended my reason!—From experience I now am qualified to be thy instructor: O my child, attend to my words, and be wise!

Indeed, I am under no great anxiety as to what thy lot may be in this world, provided thy life be virtuous.

virtuous. I hope all other good will follow: For whilst thou art virtuous, thou never wilt be forsaken of God, or totally rejected by thy fellow-creatures: Thy want of riches is in many respects freedom from temptation; such is the kindness of heaven, in that which is withheld, as well as in that which may be given. When we see good men afflicted, which frequently happen to some, during the whole course of a long life; for what can this be, but to exercise their faith, and advance them in their progress to perfection? There needs no extraordinary powers of understanding to reconcile such events. Perhaps if they had not been afflicted, they would not have retained their virtue.

I learnt in my early days, that even Heathens concluded, from the distress in which virtue is sometimes involved, and from the splendor in which vice frequently triumphs, there must be a state of rewards and punishments after death; and accordingly, my master told me, that their ancient poets represented this state in very strong and significant terms. They had no clear lights to guide them; we have such lights. No man on earth has been in heaven, or in hell, to tell us what is passing there; but the word of God gives us as much information in this matter as can possibly be necessary; for if men believe it not, "neither would they be persuaded though one should rise from the dead." Could I, my dear child, "represent to thee the different states of *good* "and *bad* men: could I give thee the prospect "which the blessed martyr ST. STEPHEN had, and "shew

"shew thee the blessed JESUS, at the right hand of
"God, surrounded with angels, and *the spirits of
"just men made perfect:* could I open thine ears to
"hear the never ceasing hymns of praise, which the
"blessed above *sing to him that was, and is, and is
"to come;* to *the lamb that was slain, but liveth for
"ever:* could I lead thee through the unbounded
"regions of eternal day, and shew the mutual and
"unbounded joys of saints, who are at rest from
"their labour, and live for ever in the presence of
"God!—Or could I change the scene, and unbar
"the iron gates of hell, and carry thee through
"solid darkness, *to the fire that never goes out,* and *to
"the worm that never dies:* could I shew thee the
"apostate angels fast bound in chains, or the souls
"of wicked men, overwhelmed with torment and
"despair: could I open thine ears to hear the deep
"itself groan with the continual cries of misery;
"cries which can never reach the throne of mercy,
"but return in sad echoes, and add even to the
"very horrors of hell!" Could I do this, my child,
I should rouse every faculty of thy soul, and arm
thee with a triple shield to guard it against the
dangers it is exposed to.

What I have been saying to thee, is not visionary
nor fanatical; they are the words of a great divine *,
drawn from the scriptures; and thou mayest plainly
perceive in them, the most nervous sense and manly
piety, devoid of all poetical fiction, and free from

DR. SHERLOCK, vol. I. discourse I.

the bitter sighs of melancholy, the false fears of superstition, or the irregular warmth of enthusiasm.

Make it thine own, by recollection; and *live*, as if thou hadst the glories of heaven in thy view! Thus, by the mercies of God, thou wilt ere long arrive in those blissful regions, which the learned and judicious prelate has so beautifully described, there to sing hallelujahs before the throne of the Almighty, in the transcendent glory of one supreme, and partake of that happiness which surpasses *all description*, and will endure *for ever and ever!*

DISCOURSE XX.

The great advantages of patience and caution in domestic service. Danger of censoriousness.

I AM under some apprehensions thou hast experienced so much tenderness under my humble roof, thou wilt think thy treatment the harsher any where else: but *fear not*; rather suspect that an excess of kindness may make thee *proud*, or lead thee into some other snare, than be discomfited, if some things should be displeasing to thee. Blessed are those who do not raise their expectations above measure, for they shall not be disappointed. Nothing is more natural to youth than impatience. Their inexperience flatters them into a belief, that every thing ought to be according to their will.

They

They forget the proverb, that "the farthest way about is the nearest way home;" and are often in so great a hurry as to defeat their own purpose. They do not accommodate their minds to others, as subordination requires, and yet they flatter themselves that others will submit to them.

Thou knowest this proverb, "hasty men never want woe;" and it is most true, that impatience often involves them in quarrels and difficulties. I charge thee to cherish love for *patience*, in imitation of thy Saviour. Carry these truths stored in thy mind. " A patient man will bear for a time, and " afterward joy shall spring up unto him. He will " hide his words for a time; and the lips of many " shall declare his wisdom. The sinner shall not " escape with his spoils; and the patience of the " godly shall not be in vain." These, my daughter, are the sentiments given in this case, by the wisest man, except one, that ever lived upon earth; and the experience of above two thousand years, has confirmed the matter.

The government of the tongue is a branch of patience, for unseemly words are a great proof of the want of it. We have a common saying of those who speak foolishly, " that a fool's bolt is soon shot." We have two ears, and but one tongue, as if providence meant that we should hear much, and speak little. To use good words is an easy obligation; but not to speak ill, requires only our silence, which costs nothing. When thou hearest evil reports, repeat them not; thou wilt be sure of doing no harm to thyself, nor injustice to thy neighbour: and this will afford thee more true satisfaction, than any pleasure thou could'st enjoy in telling a tale, the very repetition of which carries with it some degree of evil. If there is no use in telling it, but merely for conversation, there is some danger; and therefore let every one talk of it, before thou openest thy mouth; and do it then with tenderness and sorrow, rather than severity and satisfaction. There is joy in heaven over a sinner that repenteth, and shall sinful man make a play-game of human misery?— O my child, let not thy charity and compassion forsake thee, nor my lessons be given in vain. The day will come when thou wilt think them of great value; and how vastly shall I gain by thus cultivating thy heart, as well as my own, when I must leave my fields to another husbandman.

Believe me, there is nothing so dangerous or so contemptible, as a satirical vein, and an overbearing manner of treating friends or foes. "He that maketh others afraid of his wit, had need be afraid of their memory." To despise those with whom we commonly converse, or turn them into ridicule, is so ungenerous, I may say so treacherous, that it is shocking to humanity. The best dispositions have many blemishes; and why should we speak of them to no good end? The artful way of mentioning some slight merits, to gain credit for candor, and then come out with a *but,* and heavy accusations, is abominable! Always think before thou speakest.

In

In order to live peaceably " never conſtrue that in earneſt which may be conſidered as ſpoken in jeſt; and be careful not to ſay that in a jeſt which may be conſtrued in earneſt." It is proverbial, that " many a true word has been ſpoken in jeſt:" But whether it be jeſt or earneſt, people conceited of their wit, uſually ſay what they think is bright and ſhining, let it coſt them or their neighbour ever ſo dear. There is a time when *nothing*, a time when *ſomething*, but *no time* when *all things* are to be ſpoken. Life and death are in the power of the tongue: Therefore take heed, my child, of whom, and to whom, thou ſpeakeſt.

The fondneſs which moſt people have, of hearing themſelves ſpeak, and of entertaining each other, often prompts them to ſupply the defect of *memory* by *invention*; not by premeditated falſehood, but in a flow of ſpirits they make their ſtory good at all events. Moſt people who attempt to tell ſtories, are apt to tell them too often, eſpecially as they grow old! but " a tale out of ſeaſon, is as " merry muſic in mourning;" and many a good ſtory, ill told, appears as a bad one.

Above all, let me caution thee never to cloſe thine eyes in ſleep, without recollecting whether thou haſt not ſaid ſomething *wicked* or *fooliſh*, *too much*, or perchance *too little* in the day paſt. Repent, with ſhame and ſorrow. There are ſome who are ſo unguarded and liberal of ſpeech, and who indulge their reſentments ſo much, that their whole life becomes a

H ſcene

scene of folly, or guilt; and some who are so callous, they know not when they offend.

Nothing creates variance so much as an evil tongue: young persons, especially females, should take particular care, not to indulge themselves in much talking: it cannot be reconciled to modesty; and it opens such a field for familiarity, particularly among servants, as is apt to breed hatred and contempt, or love out of season. Thou mayest observe, that people of no education, are so much the less reserved in the decency and modesty of their discourse.

Consider also thy particular situation as a servant. The superior station of thy mistress will naturally lead her to expect a degree of homage from thee; and that thou should'st not speak but when thou art spoken to, and then be as ready as thou canst with thy answer. If her regard for thee should incline her sometimes to speak familiarly, never forget she is thy mistress. If she should occasionally consider thee as her humble friend, and companion, thy task will become the more difficult. If thou speakest boldly, it may be considered as impertinence; and if thou flatterest her, as is the custom of female servants in such circumstances, she being a woman of understanding, will look upon thee with contempt. In common life, we, who from birth and education, have no view beyond servitude, are apt to grow useless, if not impertinent, when we meet with much indulgence.

If thy mistress should demand thy opinion of a matter thou dost not understand, to excuse thyself
as

as being ignorant, is sufficient; but if thou art acquainted with it, relate the facts, rather than give thy opinion of them, and leave her to form a judgment, declaring in the most submissive terms, how much more able she is to judge, than thyself. This thou mayest do without the least violation of truth; for in all human probability, it will be the case; but remember to express thyself in as *few*, not in as *many* words as possible. I have said the more on this subject, not only with a view to teach thee how to behave in general, but because happiness in service depends so much on the government of the *tongue*.

DISCOURSE XXI.

The great importance of truth; and the infamy and punishment of lying.

FROM the government of the tongue, consider next, the importance of *truth*. I have heard my master say, that the Egyptians of old were used to wear a golden chain, beset with precious stones, which they stiled *truth*, intimating that to be the most illustrious ornament.

The sacred writings tell us, that *God is truth*; and therefore to pervert the use of our speech, which so remarkably distinguishes us from the beasts that perish, must be a high offence to him. " *Truth is* always consistent with itself, and needs nothing to
help

help it out: it is always at hand, and fits upon our lips, and is ready to drop out before we are aware; whereas a *lye* is troublesome, and sets a man's invention on the rack; and one trick needs a great many more to make it good." Servants are but too justly accused of being guilty of the vice of lying, yet unhappily it is not confined to them.

Among the first *christians*, they counted it a most impious thing, even to *dissemble* the truth; and when under persecution, scorned even life itself, rather than preserve it on such base terms. This was not enthusiasm, but sober sense and reason: they were followers of him " in whose lips was no guile !"

It may be thy fortune to live among people who make no scruple, occasionally, to tell each other in plain words, that *they lye*. This has a harsh sound, and a severe meaning. There are many *untruths* advanced wantonly or by mistake; in such cases do thou reply in decent terms, as *I think you are misinformed*, or, *I believe you are mistaken:* those who have any breeding, often add, *you will pardon me*, or, *you will excuse me*.

There are also many lyes of *vanity*, which are deceitful, though not intended to injure. People who are too wise to believe what is sometimes said, look serious on such occasions, and make no reply. It seems to be a duty of friendship, as well as humanity and religion, among intimates, to admonish in private for such lyes; though I am sorry to tell thee, my child, that mankind seldom have so much courage on the one side to give, or humility on the other,

other, to take such notice in a friendly way, of any sort of lyes.

Whatever the case may be, to *give the lye*, is a great fault, though thou should'st be much provoked: but it is a greater *to tell one*. Women should be at least as careful of their honour, in this instance, as men usually are. Amongst the gentry, there are some men who will tell a lye without any hesitation; but if they are reproached by another, in order to support a good name, they demand his *blood*. Thus many have fought under a notion of preserving their *honour*, who had no good name; and consequently hazarded their lives like fools, for *nothing!* I tell thee this, that thou mayest know what is passing in the world, and civilize thy manners, as all people ought to do.

My master used to say, there are some nations, whom we affect to despise for their ignorance and poverty, more civilized than ourselves; and among whom there is less danger of suffering violence. Civility, even in a carman, which we occasionally see, naturally delights, and makes one wish to be his friend; as when he is brutish, we long to see him chastised. Remember, that people who are really honest at heart, are clear in their discourse, and keep close to truth: " Lying is the vice of a villain, a coward, and a slave. All that thou canst get by lying or dissembling, is, that thou wilt not be believed when thou speakest truth." If thou tellest a lye thou wilt be tempted to support one falshood by another;

another; and a continued aggravation of guilt, or a bitter repentance muſt follow.

I am ſorry to tell thee, that there are many ſervants, now a days, who ſcruple not to *tell lies*, and others who *equivocate*, and evade the truth. They mean to ſupport a certain character, by appearing to have more virtue than they can make a juſt claim to; and yet degrade themſelves by the infamous practice of lying.

Thoſe who have been brought up in the fear of God, and underſtand the vileneſs of a lye, muſt be extremely diſtreſſed when they are taken by ſurprize; but to intend by ſuch means to deceive, is ſhocking!—Lying is a vice which walks abroad with gigantic ſtrides. It prevails much among thoſe who are in a ſtate of ſervitude, as if they were ignorant that a lye is a crime of the blackeſt die. SOLOMON ſays, " a *thief* is better than a man accuſtomed *to lye*, but they both ſhall inherit deſtruction;" and ſpeaking in his own perſon, ſays, " I have hated many things, but nothing like a *faiſe* man, for the *Lord* will hate him." Deſtroy *truth* among men, and they will become to each other, worſe than beaſts; for theſe, I believe, practiſe no deceit upon their own kind, whatever ſome which live by prey, may do on other animals.

The wiſe man ſays, " the lip of truth ſhall be eſtabliſhed *for ever*; but a lying tongue is but for a moment." All wiſe people hold their tongues when it is not proper to ſpeak; but to *lye, deceive,* or *equivocate,*

vocate, is practising in the works of the devil, who is styled the *father of lyes*.

My dear child, I hope thou wilt convince thy mistress, and thy master, if thou should'st have one, and every body else, that thou hast a soul superior to falshood, and dareft to tell the truth, to those who have a right to require it, though thou should'st condemn thyself to the severest suffering.

It is thus thou mayest be sure of respect, and perhaps of promotion; " Keep thy word, and deal faithfully, and thou shalt always find the thing that is neceffary for thee." The wife man does not engage, that dealing faithfully shall make every one rich; this would be impossible; but that it will provide every one with what is neceffary for them; which is all we can with any decency beg of the Almighty, or perhaps, with safety wish for or defire.

If I should live to hear thou hast told a lye, it will be as a dagger to my heart: All the labours of my mind in thy service, in giving thee instruction, though they will return into my own bosom, yet with regard to thee, they will be mixed with the bitterness of sorrow. Cherish in thine heart the love of *truth*: I have told thee that *God is truth*; and therefore those who love truth, *love God*, and will be beloved of him; and however mean their condition on earth may be, they are the objects of his mercy, and will be made happy for ever and ever!

DISCOURSE XXII.

The detestable qualities of pride and vain glory. Story of a miserable prostitute. On vanity, and the danger of flattery.

MY last instruction being upon the subject of truth, I will now endeavour to point out to thee the hateful nature of *pride:* Pride is apt to lurk in every human heart; consider therefore what is passing in thine own bosom. What is it such wretched mortals as we are, can be proud of? If we do well, it is but our duty. Observe how the wretched little pismire, man, struts about when he is proud! Behold what an extravagant opinion he has of his own merits; what an immoderate conceit of his own genius, and how low he holds others in esteem, who probably may be more estimable than himself. How untractable are the proud; how seldom they yield to reason; and how often they involve themselves and others in difficulties, which might have been easily avoided.

It is amazing to consider, how such *things of dust,* as men, can indulge pride: If thou feelest this passion work in thy breast, despise thyself in dust and ashes; and pity others when they are guilty.

When

When I receive a favour, done with an air of pride and disdain, it loses more than half its value; and my heart almost revolts against the expression of my gratitude, to those who deserve so little of my esteem. To be proud of knowledge is absurd, seeing that the wisest know so little: and as to riches, do not the greatest among men stand in need of the meanest? Are not *our* labours at least as useful to them, as their wealth to us?

Pride, when it exalts us in our own esteem, and tempts us to despise others, never fails to wound the peace of mortals, and frequently turns their brain. I believe there are more lunatics from pride than from any other passion. Thou hast read, that it was the crime of fallen angels. The wise man says, " the beginning of it is, when one departeth from God, and his heart is turned from his Maker:" Remember, that thou art a *christian!* a follower of the meekest and greatest personage that ever lived. Consider how the brightness of Christ's humility darts forth rays, which dazzle and confound the pride of man!

SOLOMON says, " that vengeance, as a lion, shall lie in wait for the proud; but humility and the fear of the Lord, are riches, and honour, and life." Thou seest that he considers humility as inseparable from the fear of God, and productive of worldly blessings. But he tells us, " the proud are hated of God, and as they plough iniquity, and sow wickedness, they shall reap the same."

Proud people are generally the moſt ignorant of their own hearts; nor can we ſee ourſelves, whilſt pride ſtands in our light. How many in all ſtations has it brought to ruin!

I will relate a tale which will melt thine heart! I remember a farmer's daughter in this neighbourhood, who was ſent to London, as thou art now going. A place which was thought a very good one was provided for her; but ſhe, like a ſilly girl, and impatient of controul, thought ſhe needed neither admonition nor inſtruction; and in a petulant humour gave warning to her miſtreſs. Unable to get another place ſo good, ſhe declined a worſe, which ſhe might have had, and was ſoon ſeized by the cold hand of poverty: and what was the conſequence? to relieve her wants, ſhe became a *proſtitute!* She might even then have returned to her father; but neither would her pride allow of this. He heard of her evil conduct, and wrote to her in terms that might have moved a heart of flint; at the ſame time requeſting of me to ſeek her out, and expoſtulate with her. I thought myſelf fortunate in finding her, though in a brothel. After ſome other queſtions, for I ſpoke in the ſpirit of humanity, I aſked her if ſhe believed in a future life, and in a ſtate of rewards and puniſhments after death, and if ſhe thought the ſin ſhe lived in was not forbidden by the chriſtian religion, under the penalty of everlaſting damnation, if ſhe died impenitent? She looked ſtedfaſtly at me for ſome time, as if ſhe was at a loſs what anſwer to make, and then ſaid; "You may

may tell my father, I do not mean to go on in an evil courfe." But luft had perverted her heart, and turned her eyes from heaven. Folly, even to madnefs, was become her companion: fhe perfifted in vice; and before fhe reached the age of twenty-two, fhe fell a miferable victim, and died, as fuch wretched beings frequently do, of a decay.

In general, is it not enough to humble the proudeft heart, to confider, what ficknefs, pain, age, or misfortune, may reduce us to; and that a few years muft bring us all down to the duft? Of all human blindnefs and folly, nothing can be more deplorable than pride: In the *rich*, it is one of the moft mifchievous; among the *poor*, the moft contemptible of vices. Pride will choak all thy other virtues. Among the proud themfelves, thou mayeft obferve, that they hate one another, and are the firft that complain: for though a likenefs of manners in all other inftances generally begets love, in this it produces hatred.

Confult thine own welfare: think what the effects of pride ufually are; mockery, derifion, and reproach. From the fame fountain flow unforgivenefs, cruelty, and the contempt of others. O my child, defpife not the meaneft perfon on earth: thou art duft, and unto duft fhalt thou return! Suffer not pride to hurry thee into refentments of the untoward behaviour of others. At firft view, it feems to be difficult to return *good* for *evil*, but thou haft been taught from thy youth up, that this is wifdom and virtue, and immortal glory! How many through pride, shew the fiercest resentments for mere trifles.

Thou wilt be told, perhaps, that a portion of pride is necessary for a woman, and the best preservative of her chastity: But such advisers mistake a reserve of behaviour, which often proceeds from a principle of prudence, for that detestable vice. This reserve thou wilt generally do well to practise, but do not confound so obvious a distinction as many are apt to do.

Vanity and *affectation* are vices to which thy sex is in a particular manner addicted; it is necessary therefore to give thee a caution against them. Vanity is the folly of foolishness; and affectation, the cryer that proclaims it. If thou meanest to preserve thyself pure, and untainted, dread vanity! When a woman grows vain of the charms of her person, her fine cloaths, or accomplishments, she exposes herself to ridicule, and as it were, invites temptation: for who expects resistance from those who have so little understanding?

One would not imagine, child, that in our rank of life, these vices should ever be seen; but there are fools of all sorts; and I have seen young women in villages, as well as heard of them in courts, whom the looking-glass, or the flattery of men, have perverted, even so as to turn their brains; and I believe the consequences of purity are generally the most fatal, in the lower state of life.

They are more dangerously ill, who are drunk with vanity, than those who are intoxicated with wine.

wine. In the last case, a short time sobers them again; but in the former they sometimes become incorrigible; and thou mayest be assured, that every woman is defective in understanding, in the same degree that she abounds in vanity.

Take care, my child, how thou trustest to *flatterers*. The greater the commendation is, the more be thou on thy guard, and do not fall a sacrifice to a few empty words, though there should be some truth in them. Believe not all the good that is spoken of thee, whether it be said to thy face or not.

" 'The only advantage of flattery, regarding virtue or understanding, is, that by hearing what we are not, we may be instructed in what we ought to be:" I have heard my master observe, that it is a very *old saying* " that flatterers never lift any one up, but as the eagle does the tortoise, to get something by his fall; and that crows devour only the dead, but flatterers the living."

On the other hand, it is most true, " that in the fulness of the heart the mouth speaketh," and some kind and tender words will fall from honest tongues, which if not all strictly true, do not the less proceed from the heart.——However, shut thine ears to flattery, whatever quarter it may come from.

As to us men, we are lavish in the praises of women, whose personal charms make impressions on us; but be cautious how thou listenest, lest thou should'st fall, where thou apprehendest no danger,

DISCOURSE XXIII.

On envy. Malice. Revenge. Cunning. Anecdote of a girl who lost her lover by discovering her propensity to envy.

IN all thy steps consider the honour of God, and the care of thine own soul. *Pride* and *vanity* lead to *envy:* Weak and wicked minds have often committed horrible crimes from mere envy: The envious poison themselves with the virtues of others. SOLOMON says, " the envious man hath a wicked eye, he turneth away his face, and despiseth men."

The surest sign of a generous and good disposition, is to be without envy: but the base and ignoble are generally envious. In all the catalogue of vices, none seem to be more foolishly wicked and abominable, than *envy*, except *malice* and *revenge*. To pretend to lessen what we will not imitate, or to wish to humble those above us, because they are above us, has something in it so black, that I know not how to express the hatred which thou oughtest to have of it. Other passions may claim a pretence, at least to some pleasure or satisfaction; but what can *envy* furnish, but pain and vexation, at that which is properly the subject of joy?

Malice is nearly related to envy, and in its effects yet more abominable: what is said of the one, may

with-

without much injustice be imputed to the other. And thou mayest constantly observe, that those who are most inclined to do any injury, are for the same reason most disposed to *malice*; or in other words, least willing to forgive. If thou should'st at any time so far turn thine eyes from heaven, as to feel the impressions of *malice* in thine heart, look into thine own bosom and *tremble!*—O my dear child, I can say nothing stronger, than that *malice* is fit only for the ministers of the prince of darkness.

Envy and malice are the genuine offspring of Lucifer, but *revenge* is his favourite child. This passion is most apt to arise in persons of little minds, and to indulge it is equally *foolish* and *devilish*. Learn to bear an injury; and consider an affront, rather as injurious to the party who is guilty, than to thyself, being not guilty. If thy forbearance triumphs over the offence, thou art really the better, not the worse for the affront; for remember that it costs more to revenge injuries, than to bear them. I know a recent instance in which this passion was gratified: but it cost the party very dear. A girl of this neighbourhood taking offence, robbed a man of his bride, by telling a story which was not true, or very much disguised. When the truth came out, it occasioned her losing her own lover, who was too generous in his nature, to bear the thoughts of an alliance with a woman so dangerous with her tongue.

Thou knowest, that our divine religion commands us to be charitable and tender, even to our enemies, and

and to do them *good* when they do us *evil*. Solomon was a Jew, yet he says, " He that *revengeth* shall *find vengeance* from the Lord, and he will *surely keep his sins in remembrance.*" What then will become of such a miserable being, if because of his revenge, his sins shall be *had in remembrance* against *him?* Can we recollect too often that he that hateth his neighbour cannot love his God? We are likewise admonished to be kind to others, tender-hearted, *forgiving*, as we hope for Christ's sake to be forgiven.

Cunning is also a crime, and one that is imputed most to thy sex, and to the very worst part of it, who are often dupes to their own deceit. Thou mayest have heard of an *artful woman*, or in other words, a *cunning woman*, who has the talent of deceiving, or taking the advantage of the ignorance or simplicity of other people. Cunning is sometimes mistaken for wisdom, but is really as different from it as light is from darkness. Wisdom is truth itself—but cunning is a lye artfully insinuated, with a view to deceive, from an idea that if truth be disguised, the purpose will be answered.

I must also warn thee of the danger of *credulity*, or being too forward in *believing*, whether the matter relates to thyself or others. Consider *what* is said, and *by whom* it is said; compare it with thy experience; examine how far thy belief may concern thy interest; how it may hurt thy charity, or affect thy person. Nothing will sooner induce thee to believe a man, than when he commends thee;

nothing

nothing ought to alarm thee so much. Many a poor girl has fallen a sacrifice to the ready credit which she gave to the high commendations of her personal charms. If we examine the nature of praise in general, the partiality of some, and the inability of others to judge, there is great danger of its being often bestowed in the wrong place. What a bustle have we heard made by the multitude, in praise perhaps of the vainest, or most vicious person; whilst for want of virtue in themselves, or common discernment, they have totally over-looked the most virtuous characters!

DISCOURSE XXIV.

The danger of an eager pursuit of pleasure. On amusements, choice of company, and conversation, as the safeguard of life.

BE on thy guard, let me warn thee, my child, against the danger of an eager pursuit after pleasure:—Think, what fools those are, who give themselves up to idle gratifications, which are so short in themselves, and so often attended with bitter repentance, or endless torments! Let me tell thee a fable: A boy, greatly smitten with the colours of a butterfly, pursued it from flower to flower, with indefatigable pains; first he aimed to surprize it among the leaves of a rose; then to cover it with

his

his hat, as it was feeding on a daisy; now hoped to secure it, as it rested on a sprig of myrtle; and then grew sure of his prize, perceiving it loiter on a bed of violets. But the fickle fly continually changing one blossom for another, still eluded his attempts. At length observing it half buried in the cup of a tulip, he rushed forward, and snatching it with violence, crushed it to pieces. The dying insect seeing the poor boy chagrined at his disappointment, addressed him in the following manner: " Behold now, the end of thy unprofitable solicitude! and learn, for the benefit of thy future life, that all pleasure is but a painted butterfly; which although it may serve to amuse thee in the pursuit, if embraced with too much ardour, will perish in the grasp."

No man is a master of himself so long as he is a slave to any thing else. Reason grows stronger by the exercise of it; and does not the love of vicious pleasures acquire strength by the indulgence of them? Thou perhaps mayest think it more in character for *me* to *preach*, than for *thee* to *practise*. It is true, that I am in the decline of life, but for the same reason that I have travelled through it, I am the better able to inform thee, not only of the best roads, but also how to guard against falling from the precipices, or sinking into the quick-sands with which it abounds.

I have observed how the desire of pleasure creates secret wishes and expensive pursuits; how it involves its votaries in difficulties; how often these depart
from

from their true interest, and at once sacrifice their virtue, and their happiness, to an idol, which at length falls down upon them, and destroys them. Scenes of expence and jollity, are frequently scenes of distress and misery; and *company keeping*, as *we* term it, has hurried many a young woman and man also into destruction.

I have heard some of my neighbours comfort themselves on their death beds, that they never were *company-keepers*; the very thing itself, *in their opinion*, and as they saw others abuse the liberty of modest conversation, implying a degree of guilt. On occasions of jollity, people seldom know what they are about: They warm their blood with liquor, and by the means of music and noise, they banish reflection; and the consequences which often follow are dreadful.

Our great philosopher and friend, says, " The heart of the wise is in the house of mourning; but the heart of the fool is in the house of mirth;" teaching us that *wise men* rather go where they can do *some real good*, and shudder not at beholding the most serious parts of life; but that *fools* consider only how they shall be diverted: and you may observe the aversion of a great part of mankind to serious scenes, and things that require thought.

Beware of the danger of amusement at improper times, and in doubtful company. All the world knows, that the fine lady and the country lass, equally delight in *dancing* and *singing*; the difference is only in the manner. Now let me advise thee to
avoid

avoid both, in company; *singing* is an amusement, and may be indulged in *private:* but *idle songs* are apt to ensnare; especially if thou should'st happen to excel thy companions. I have known this happen in many cases, both of the young and middle aged, men and women. The best application of a good voice is in psalmody.

As to *dancing*, it is never practised but in company; and *in our station, dancing company* is, I think, generally bad company. Dancing, among us, is hardly ever conducted with perfect decency, and freedom from danger to young persons; particularly young women. I know not if *dancing* be worse in town or country, but there is no necessity to declare against it, in such terms as to quarrel with thy neighbours, who resolve to *dance* at all hazards. These are the occasions when such young persons are *least* on their guard, and when men of evil intentions are *most* on the watch, to carry their wicked designs on girls into execution. I wish that thou, my child, should'st be amused by *walking*, or any thing innocent, *when thou art permitted to amuse thyself*, rather than by *dancing*. Thou wilt always find amusement and instruction, in *reading*, provided thou makest choice of good and proper books, otherwise there is mischief also.

Great care is necessary in the choice of companions. Be assured that wherever the speech is impure, the mind is corrupted. If thou meanest to preserve thyself untainted, it is time to withdraw when the discourse is *wicked, indecent,* or *slanderous*. Consider thy companions in a great measure, as

good

good or bad, according as they are tender or cruel toward their neighbour. Always endeavour to change the subject, when others are ill spoken of. Soften the rigour of the sentence given by them, and avoid injustice towards a good name, as thou would'st decline *theft* or *robbery*. If thou art satisfied from circumstances that the party absent is injured, plead their cause with a becoming warmth. In acting thus thou wilt do as thou would'st be done by.

Endeavour to accommodate thyself to the condition of those with whom thou conversest. If they are in a *higher* condition than thyself, the more silence and attention will be necessary: with those who are *lower*, the more affability will be proper. Never affect being so much above the *meanest* as to treat them with insolence. But whether *superiors*, *equals*, or *inferiors*, if they are viciously inclined, avoid them: do it with as much decency as thy circumstances will admit of: but still I say, *avoid them*. The very " *hatred* of the vicious will do thee less harm than their *conversation*." Remember, that it's the second word that makes the quarrel, and that the injurer is generally the last that forgives.

In thy intercourse with the world, " be not captious, nor given to contradiction, for this occasions contention; nor be rudely familiar, for this breeds contempt. If any thing be not *fitting*, do it not: If it be not *true*, speak it not." Our tempers are frequently more easily discovered in little circumstances, than in great ones: True *Christians* strive to keep their temper on all occasions without any unbecoming

becoming warmth. Thou rememberest when the disciples of our Saviour were in a flame of resentment against the *Samaritans*, he rebuked them by saying, " Ye know not what spirit ye are of."

An obliging disposition, will always engage the attention of *superiors*; and take heed, my child, that as *thou* wouldst think it cruel to be condemned as *ill-natured*, for being sometimes off thy guard, or out of humour, so as to express a hasty peevishness, do not expect perfection in others.

This instruction is more particularly necessary in thy station; for as servants are more ready to make remarks on this subject, than masters imagine they do; themselves should likewise be the more attentive to their own conduct, not to offend.

DISCOURSE XXV.

Generosity. Charity. Character of Mrs. Ann Saracen. Reflections on it. Ability to do good in the humblest fortune.

AS I am giving thee rules for thy general conduct in life, remember that *generosity* ceases to be a virtue, when it entices us to do offices of kindness beyond our power. Our virtues, as expressed in action, must be suited to our circumstances. The mind may retain a readiness of disposition to serve others, and so far be as fruitful as the rain which

cometh

cometh down from the heavens: but where there is no water in the clouds, none can fall upon the earth. Whatever is in thy power, let it flow from a free hand, and an open heart. The humblest actions sometimes carry with them a greatness of mind, superior even to the bounties of kings; and we must be contented when it pleases providence to restrain us with regard to the means of relieving others; and think with gratitude of the relief we receive ourselves, still maintaining the generosity of our minds.

The more prudent thou art, the more able thou wilt always be to assist those who are in particular distress. Every one has some power; and as the widow's mite was considered by the Son of God, as a great charity, thy little contribution may be useful to the afflicted, and acceptable in his sight, who sees the heart. If it happens, that thou hast *nothing* which thou canst spare, God will accept the thoughts of thine heart. A *tear* offered up to misery, where only a tear can flow, will be pleasing to the tender Father of mankind, who in such cases accepts the will for the deed. It is better to be of a generous mind, and of the number of those who stand in need of relief, than of a hard-hearted disposition, though in plenty.

When you can do it with a probability of success, and with good manners, forget not that it is as essential a part of charity, to warn people of danger to their souls, as it is to preserve their bodies.

These

These are duties clearly deducible from the uniform conduct of our Saviour.

The same charity, which among christians makes men humble, just, and watchful to do all the good, and avoid all the evil possible, makes them also courteous and obliging. And nothing can be more certain, than that one may be very charitable without having any thing to give: and very *uncharitable*, and yet, as St. *Paul* says, give ones body to be burned.

Charity, as comprehending *christian love*, is so absolutely commanded, and is truly so much the bond of society, that the neglect of it can never be dispensed with. And what can exceed the *pleasure* of seeing others made happy, except the making them so by our own means? By taking a share in the miseries of others, we render wretchedness the more supportable; whereas plenty, amidst the frowns and contempt of the world, is but a splendid kind of misery. The *miser* is, of all characters in the world, the most hated. There are various ways of being charitable, besides giving money; but in that respect much may be done by a moderate fortune, where self-denial is practised, and the heart sincere.

Thou hast often heard me talk of *Ann Saracen*; she lives in a cottage of three pounds annual rent, but it is as neat and as clean as any palace. When she dines at home, she feeds on the value of about three-pence: she eats and drinks of any wholsome aliment that comes in her way; but with such moderation, she never hurts her health by excess. From long experience, she understands the quality of many drugs,

drugs, and the use of kitchen physic; dispensing the former with great judgment and success —By the superiority of her understanding, she is able to instruct her poor neighbours, influencing their conduct by reason, and the books which she gives them to read.—She visits prisons, and converses with condemned malefactors.—She puts children to school, and employs them in needle-work, partly by making up old linen which she begs of her rich acquaintance:—This she again devotes to the use of the indigent, by assisting them with child-bed linen; which is returned clean to her after it hath been used, and the same things serve for the birth of many children. All this is performed within the bounds of forty pounds a year.

Thus amidst the checks of a scanty fortune, she acts like a gentlewoman and a christian; shining like a star, to guide the poor, the afflicted, and the weary, to rest and comfort. When you praise her for her good deeds, she contracts herself like the sensitive plant, constantly referring whatever is excellent to God, who is the only true fountain of all excellence.

She says, "What do I that every christian woman "who is mistress of her time and fortune would not "do? If I am so happy as to have the favour of "my superiors, I lay them under an obligation, "when I offer them an opportunity of doing good. "He that neglects such an occasion defraudeth his "own soul. If I plead the cause of poor creatures "who dare not appear to speak for themselves, I

"am so far an advocate in the cause of heaven, and
"act as a steward to the family of God. I must
"use the talents my master hath entrusted me with;
"and when I have done give the glory to that
"being who is graciously pleased to make me the
"instrument of his mercy. In this view I think
"myself preferred to a higher employment, than if
"I were first lady of the bed-chamber to the queen.
"If the fine world is infatuated with such trifles as
"dress and diversion, and make these the business
"of their lives; if the gay are carried on, as it
"were by a resistless stream, swimming on the sur-
"face in a delightful phrenzy, careless of the gulph
"which may swallow them up; what can I do
"more than send up my petitions to the throne of
"grace, that their eyes may be opened to see their
"danger, and that recovering their strength, they
"may get on shore in safety, if it shall please the
"Almighty to avert his judgments? The world
"will be governed by appearances—happy are
"those who discern realities."

What dost thou think of this character? is it not charming? Such should we all be, if we were practically *christians!* I often think, when I take my rounds amongst my sick and poor neighbours, whose wants are greater than I can relieve, if they to whom providence has given affluence, would accustom themselves to be spectators of the miseries of vast numbers below them, they would surely sacrifice a little more to humanity and charity, and would not offer quite so much incense to the lust of

the

the eye, and the pride of life. The time is drawing nigh, when attainments in holiness will alone be of any avail, and when those who have " turned many to righteousness will shine as the stars for ever and ever!" Be assured that all which has not obedience to God for its object, is full of vanity and delusion.

Thy mistress is admirably inclined to offices of piety and humanity: Entreat her leave to inform her, of whatever thou knowest, in regard to misery and distress: She will judge of what she ought to do. She will not withhold her bread from the fatherless, who are dying with hunger; nor behold those who are perishing for want of cloathing, expire at her gates: She will not make gold her confidence: The land will not cry against her, nor the furrows thereof complain; but she will have mercy on the poor! Forget not, that charity will endure when time itself shall cease!—O my child, the earth, and all that we see of the objects around us, even the heavens which are the canopy of it, will pass away! Faith will be swallowed up in sight, and hope cease with enjoyment: but charity is so divine and pure in its nature, it will constitute part of the joys of heaven.

DISCOURSE XXVI.

Duty of learning to read. Reading the scriptures essential to religion.—On writing.—Frugality.—Prudence.—Fable of the wolf and the lamb.—On modesty.—Bashfulness.

IT is sometimes a question among our superiors, whether people of the lower classes are the better for being taught to read. If reading were universal it could not create any distinction. In this free country, where women have the same privileges as men, they may with the same propriety be taught to read.

The men who do the hard labour and drudgery of life, are not the most instructed; and therefore it becomes the more beneficial to a family that a wife should be able to assist the husband. If she is in any degree qualified to instruct her children, whilst the father is in the field, she will save so much, and probably teach them better than any old woman in the neighbourhood could do.

We are *commanded to read the scriptures,* and for the same reason, obliged to teach our children to read: if all of us were so taught, no one could pretend to be above laborious employments; for we should know from the word of God, that labour is the condition of human life. The knowledge which

is

is the glory of the human race, is within the compass of us all. It is contained in the New Testament: but how shall we know what is there unless we read? We may hear it read by parts at church, but it cannot be supposed to make the same impression as when the book is before us, and we may read it through in our own way, consider it verse by verse, compare our lives by it, and refer all our hopes and views to it, by the conformity of our practice. All that the finest writers or most learned men have ever said, or can say concerning social duties, and the beauty of virtue, must come to this: Is our conduct agreeable to the word of God? Shall we do as we are commanded? Can any motive to any action be higher than the love and obedience we owe to God? Can we find any rewards so great as those he hath promised?

The great end of learning, my dear child, " is to know God, and out of that knowledge to love and obey him." Thou wilt perceive, that in most instances which concern God, we cannot carry our thoughts so high, or find language proper to express them, but as we borrow words from sense. The scriptures, which were written for our learning, speak of the anger and the love, the hands and the eyes of God; but we are to guard against gross conceptions, as we know that God is a spirit, not visible to mortal eyes, infinite in purity, and devoid of passion. The wisdom which the scriptures teach will avail us, when all the learning that our superiors can boast of, if not applied to the same purposes,

poses, or made a bad use of, will leave them in a much worse condition than if they had remained in the grossest ignorance.

However necessary reading may be for learning our duty to our maker, the same cannot be said of writing. It seems reasonable, in our rank and condition, that women should be taught to write rather than men; and the more, as the duties of a shop may in general be as well performed by a woman as a man. In any case a woman may be of equal service to receive or pay; take in or deliver out by weight or measure; but in general women cannot act the part of sailors or soldiers, nor do the business of ploughmen, carpenters, smiths, or bricklayers.

" *Prudence* is an universal virtue, which enters into the composition of all the rest: Judgment is its throne, and silence its sanctuary."—Young people are generally more prodigal than old ones. Whether thou hast little or much, take care of it, and do not expend it in vanity: money may stand thy friend, when others fail thee. The caution holds stronger for them who have but little, than for those who have a great deal. In money affairs, remember that " often counting makes good friends."

Charity seems to forbid our mistrusting, prudence requires diffidence and caution; there can be no doubt, but that it would be madness to trust those with thy goods, or thy person, who shew no fear of God, nor respect for the laws of their country. Let them talk as they please, " *deeds* are fruit; *words* are

are but leaves." The more lavish such persons are in their promises, the less they are to be depended on.

The innocent silly lamb in the fable, was so credulous, that the wolf persuaded him he did not feed on flesh, as was vulgarly imagined, but on green pastures; "why then, says the lamb, we may as well feed together," and creeping from within his inclosure, joined the wolf—to be devoured, as thou mayest easily imagine. I am sorry to tell thee, that it is no strange thing for some people to put on the disguise of piety and religion, the better to ensnare those, who being honest and upright themselves, think well of the rest of mankind.

Women, who are really modest, never make a boast of *modesty*, for that is in effect being immodest. A true sense of shame is founded on virtue, for we ought to blush in secret, even at a thought which religion condemns. Cultivate such purity of mind as may render thee acceptable to him to whose eyes thy heart is open. Whatever thy company may be, take care not to offend against modesty, by any word or action: and avoid giving any smile of approbation, when words of a double meaning are spoken; and still more if they are in direct terms indecent. Jest not against the rules of good manners; rather study how to be useful to thy friends and companions, than how to divert them: Solid sense is preferable to wit; the first is always beneficial, the last seldom fails to be dangerous.

The wise man says, "If thou be invited of a mighty man, withdraw thyself, and so much the more will he invite thee;" intimating that modesty towards superiors is the ready way to be treated with respect. In the same manner when thou art conscious of ignorance, or when prudence forbids thee to speak, talking will at once discover thy want of sense, as well as want of modesty.

"A great distrust of oneself, produces fear, which depriving the mind of its liberty, makes our reasonings weak, our words trembling, and our actions faint." And it is observed, that there is the same difference between *assurance*, considered as a reasonable confidence in what we say or do, and *impudence*; as between true modesty and bashfulness.

Those who desire to do what is commendable, and yet from bashfulness cannot shew themselves to the world; ought not to be angry with it, if others, less deserving, promote their fortune in a more effectual manner.

DISCOURSE XXVII.

The advantages of friendship. Caution in respect to it. Necessity of circumspection in love.

ENTER into no connection without considering the end, how far it may please or offend God, on whom an eternity of bliss or misery depends. Friendship being the strongest obligation to the practice of virtue, as it regards particular persons, and

and the greatest comfort amidst the various calamities of life, whatever thy fortune may otherwise be, I hope thou wilt find a friend: but as there are not many who have sense and virtue enough to be capable of friendship, therefore be careful with whom thou contractest an intimacy.

Sincerity of heart, and freedom of behaviour often pass for friendship: but to be a friend, it is necessary to have a good temper, and a steadiness of mind, with such a degree of knowledge, as may enable one to give and take advice. Friends mutually compassionate each other, and they must render themselves a mutual support. They should never say or do any thing harshly, when the same thing can be done with tenderness. If thou should'st ever have a friend, avoid all such kind of discourse in company, as may undervalue the person, though it should exalt thyself. Do not presume on any friendship so far, as to use words of contempt or derision, lest thou shalt give wounds, which may not be so easily healed.

Thou wilt easily judge how rarely such are to be found, to whom we may open our hearts without reserve, and without danger. "A faithful friend is a strong defence, and he that hath found such a one, hath found a treasure." Friendship, such as we frequently find among virtuous persons, lightens our sorrows, and increases our joys; warns us in danger, and delivers us in distress. The wealth of the world, cannot fill up the measure of our wishes for a partner in our hearts; such wishes being implanted in our nature. Solomon says, "all flesh consorteth according to kind, and a man will cleave to *his like*." Death itself hath been sought in friendship, and one hath contended with another, desiring to die himself to preserve his friend. Women are most famed for *love*, men for *friendship*.

A slight acquaintance is apt to lead the unwary into intimacies, which often prove deadly in their consequences. Nothing is so dangerous as the *pretended friendship* of bad people: I say *pretended friendship*, for that which is real cannot exist upon bad principles. The council and advice of persons of superior knowledge and virtue, and whom thou hast reason to believe are sincerely interested for thy welfare, should make thee ambitious of rendering thyself worthy of their esteem, and perhaps in the issue these will prove thy best friends.

Solomon tells thee, "Love thy friend and be faithful unto him, but if he betray thy secrets, follow no more after him, for he is as a roe escaped out of the snare:" Shame, or fear of thy resentment, will make him fly thee. Disclosing a secret, under circumstances of the greatest temptation, will make a breach; but it may be closed by great repentance on one side, or great compassion on the other.

As to friendship with a person of a blemished character, shun it, or thou wilt be suspected of entertaining the same sentiments. Young persons are warm in their intimacies, and apt to shew more distinction

tinction to each other, as friends, than is consistent with civility to the rest of the world; such appearances should likewise be avoided.

If thou shouldest happen to break with thy friend, shew thy sorrow by thy silence; and not like a silly faithless creature, blab out all thou knowest. This is as wicked as it is weak, since thou wert trusted on thine honour, without any condition. Let such do as they please; be thou fixed as a rock, that stands the utmost force of dashing waves, or storms and tempests.

My dear child, observe these rules! Be slow in chusing a friend, and slower still to change: Be courteous to all; intimate with few: Slight none for their low condition, nor esteem any for their wealth and greatness.—Be not surprised nor dismayed to hear plausible excuses, from those who are unwilling to do thee a service, if on the presumption of friendship thou should'st venture to ask a kindness: In no case owe an obligation to one whom thou believest to be wicked: Never suppress that tenderness, with which a good heart naturally overflows, when those whom thou hast ever esteemed, are in real distress.

Love, when supported by the *judgment*, seems to include *friendship:* but in regard to friendship between the sexes, in youth it is rarely to be found, without a mixture of love on one side or the other: I mean that tenderness, which is so natural to the heart.

Among persons of advanced years, the flame may be so gentle and lambent as to change its name: as in extreme old age friendship itself, seems to expire. With the loss of memory, and recollection, the sensibility of distinctions ceases. Thus we are taught, in a kind of regular gradation, calmly to resign all our friendships and our loves, with every other interest in this world. But I believe that the pleasure of friendship in good minds, is the last that leaves us, except the *more solid satisfaction, the hopes of happiness after death*.

As I would not omit any subject in which thou mayest be interested, I will put thee yet more on thy guard with respect to *love*; for as this is well or ill directed, it may render thee happy or miserable. Those who become wretched by this affection, plead that other passions are for the most part of a malignant kind: but let me tell thee, when the mind is infected with love, there is nothing so serious or comic, so generous or base, which may not directly, or remotely proceed from it. The proverb says, " Follow love and it will flee thee: Flee love and it will follow thee." If this teaches modesty, it also informs us that there is much folly and caprice in love. When we ascribe to the persons beloved, qualities they do not possess, we in effect fall in love with the creature of our own brain; and this I take to be no uncommon case.

In our ordinary acquaintance, and yet more in our friendships, it is hardly possible but that the persons and conversation of some people, should be
more

more pleasing and delightful to us, than those of others; but to be unhappy, because we are not in the company of a particular person, is at once a proof of love, and not less of the weakness of that heart, the pleasures of which are so narrowly circumscribed.

It is not uncommon for a woman to imagine herself the object of a man's love, whether she desires to be so or not; as vain men often mistake the civilities of women for love. Thou, my child, mayest be subject to a double assault, either by the reality of thy affection, or the vanity of a man: and as a great part of my sex, in our rank particularly, is not remarkable for *honesty in love*, thou should'st be so much the more suspicious, and doubly on thy guard.

Nothing is so common in love, as believing absurdities which favour the passion, except the lavish professions which are made on such occasions; and from hence arises the danger. The language of passion may sometimes express the integrity of the heart, yet it is not to be trusted without great caution: and they who make no preparation for a retreat, in case of danger, may be obliged to surrender at discretion; and find themselves at length in the hands of an enemy, instead of a friend. Remember that nothing is more dangerous, in thy condition, than the unjust accusations of a *wicked man*, except the professions of his love, by which he may shew forth his highest insolence.

How-

However blameable many an honest heart has been, in giving way to affections, yet being really honest, they have smiled at sorrow and disappointment, even in the agonies of death, rather than do any thing which virtue forbids.

People of the best understanding, retain impressions longest, and often carry them to the grave. The most benevolent seem to be the most susceptible of love, and therefore should be most upon their guard. Love, as an affection of the soul, which enlarges and improves the mind, holds affinity with *augels*; as an appetite of the body, it is common to *brutes*. True love hath its root in virtue. Constancy is united with it; and where it subsists in the married state, adversity cannot divide it from the heart: it becomes a part of our nature.

True modesty is equal in both sexes; but by the custom of the world, women are obliged to be the most reserved in the discovery of their affections; whether this be an advantage or not I cannot tell.

Advice is seldom welcome when it crosses a favourite inclination; but is it not far better to feel a short pain in breaking off a dangerous treaty, than to be punished severely all our lives, for believing too well without proof, or against it?

The foolish and wicked of both sexes generally consort together, and are mutually influenced by each other. Many a young fellow goes to the gallows from being connected with bad women!

A man or woman of a profligate character, can never be a true friend to love whatever a distempered

pered imagination may suggest. The folly of such love will be as great, and probably more bitter in its consequences, than if thou wert to fix thine heart upon a man so much superior in condition, as to afford thee no prospect of being united to him. He who is out of thy reach, or him by whom thou would'st probably lose by gaining, are to be avoided with the same care.

Thou hast heard of some young women, and perhaps a few young men also, who despairing of an union with their beloved object, or in a fit of phrenzy, have done some desperate violence on themselves. Is not this converting love into a child of the devil? Whether madness be created by a raging fever, or a fit of love, it is still madness: And whether it be in love or hatred, if we trespass against heaven, we must be punished.

Love having nothing to do with pomp, our humble condition is less subject to deceit than that of the rich, for people naturally follow affection when they are poor; and those who have no wealth, nor ever had any prospect of living in affluence, have reason to hope they may support love without any other aids than health, industry, and virtue: and it seems to be more in favour of love, to have no want but of money, than to want every thing but money.

DISCOURSE XXVIII.

Warning against seducers to prostitution.—Danger of going to London.—Of being fond of fine cloaths.—Duty of chastity on Christian principles.—Danger of listening to superiors in fortune.—Melancholy story of Caroline

IN all thy steps think of the homage due to thy Maker; and the guardianship of thy soul under his Providence! Sorry I am to be constrained to tell thee, but it is necessary thou should'st know the truth: There are such vile wretches of both sexes, on this fair earth, as blushes the heavenly face of modesty to think of. Like the devil, they go about seeking whom they may devour; and when they have accomplished their foul ends, they laugh at the misery they have created, and spurn at the object they have deluded into destruction. Some even traffic in sin, and blot the most beautiful workmanship of heaven, with such hideous stains as might draw tears from the stony rock. These evil spirits in human form, flatter and promise, and swear as prodigally, as if they were to gain heaven; and are as false as hell, from whence their deceitful speeches come: They present the flattering shew of pleasure before the heedless eyes of young persons, and draw them on till they fall into the pit of destruction.

These

These enemies to virtue attempt boldly to persuade, that things which are really the worst in the world are the best. Little regarding the curse denounced against those who call evil good, and good evil, they practise the arts of the devil, when under a specious disguise he deceived our first parents. A small portion of sense and reason might shew the fallacy of all arguments, hopes, or expectations, in favour of actions which are contrary to virtue and sound religion. Listen not to them, but remember, that " virtue which parleys, is near a surrender, be it in man or woman."

Well do I remember some of my good neighbour's daughters, whom nothing would please but going up to *London*, as if they were sure of making their fortunes. Some of them have lived virtuously, both in the single and married state, and have succeeded in the world; but it hath fared ill with several of the most distinguished for beauty. For as soon as they arrived in town, they fell into the snares of those *abandoned procuresses*, who under a pretence of getting them good places, brought them like birds to the net, or lambs to the slaughter; witness ————, and ————, and others, who did not use the precaution before they left their parents, to correspond with such friends in town as they might trust themselves with, till proper places could be provided for them. It is impossible that thou should'st suspect half the wicked arts which are played off to seduce young females. I must also caution thee, that in all cases, but particularly if thou should'st
apply

apply to a *public register office*, to inform thyself exactly of the character of the person who proposes to take thee as a servant, and not less of those who give them characters.

I charge thee likewise, as thou lovest thy soul, not to indulge any desire of being *gaudily attired*. If thou shouldest feel thine heart incline to this vanity, get thyself cured of it, as a disease, which if neglected would prove mortal. Childish as this passion is, I know that it hath been the ruin of thousands, and it may tempt thee to forget those lessons, which I have sought so anxiously to imprint on thy heart. From the moment thou fixest thy fancy on dressing like a lady, I shall tremble, lest thy destruction should be at hand. What has been the fate of those who seek the trappings of folly as the wages of iniquity? What numbers of young women, without any other inclinations to wickedness, have been undone by the immoderate love of *dress* and *diversions*. Multitudes of young women accomplish their own destruction by the force of this restless vanity.

Among abandoned women, I can tell thee, that intemperance and disease bring on consumptions and decay, and few of them live beyond the age of twenty-five. Alas, my child, how deplorably do those fall, of both sexes, who offer themselves as it were sacrifices at the altars of vice and impurity!

In all conditions, remember that christianity requires nothing at our hands more clearly, or in a stronger manner, than chastity: and this consists in a fixed abhorrence of all forbidden sensual indulgence:

gence:—in a resolute guard over our thoughts and passions:—in a firm abstinence from the most distant occasions of lust and wantonness:—in a consciousness, or deep sense of the perfect holiness of God, and of his being present every where. It likewise consists in a conviction of the certain truths of our religion; and that there can be no hope of salvation where this virtue is not cherished. Therefore be not entangled in the snares of deceitful lusts, for these do confessedly " *war against the soul*;" and if this is conquered all is lost!

It is common for mankind to shelter themselves under the flimsy covering of numbers committing sin; as if corporeal punishments, or ignominious death, were the less evils, because crouds of malefactors are annually condemned to a loathsome prison, or the gallows!

I charge thee, my child, to be watchful of thy words: Unguarded conversation generally opens the door to mischief: It looks like a design to throw down the barrier of chastity. From the moment thou permittest any man to be thy confident, or allowest thyself to converse with him alone, except where there is an honourable and suitable treaty approved of by thy friends, it is most natural to conclude, there is danger. On the other hand, thou must exercise some skill in thy reserve, not to appear prudish, and subject thyself to ridicule.

People of fortune generally observe a more strict decorum, than the condition of servitude for the most part admits of; domestics therefore stand in
need

need of the greater caution. But without any comparison of conditions, build thy prudence on this great principle; that human nature is frail; that religion doth not keep the generality of men in awe, in any degree equal to what might be reasonably expected; that rich men are apt to presume on the humble condition of poor girls, to mark them as their prey; not considering that the soul of a chambermaid is as valuable as the soul of a queen.

If thou art wise, let not thy fancy loose to think of tying the knot for life, with any man above a farmer, or a tradesman, who is honest and not weak. If any gentleman should honestly or dishonestly commend thy person, let it pass as words which he may be accustomed to speak. In the first case it may be his real opinion; but he had better have concealed it in the dust. At all events guard thyself by shutting thine ears, and fly from the snare.

The generosity of men in this case is not to be trusted. I can tell thee a tragical story of this kind, in which I acted a considerable part. The daughter of a yeoman of reputation in this county was seduced by a young gentleman; he had promised to marry her, and she depended upon his *honour*. Her father was my old acquaintance, and intreated me to talk to him. I made him a visit, and amongst a variety of arguments told him, that he did not know the mischief he had done! adding, " I have heard her mournful tale; I have seen the rising sobs that shake her soul: her father's pillow is wet with briny tears; and her fond mother's cheeks redden with shame,

whilst

whilst indignation prevents the utterance of her griefs!—O shame! shame!—that a man should fawn and flatter, and mean—what shall I say?—mean to be a villain!—You will pardon me, Sir—That men in such cases act like villains you must grant. What is the pleasure which is dyed so deep in guilt, and creates so much pain and sorrow!"

He told me he would make her a proper allowance, but could not possibly think of marrying her, as he should disoblige his friends, and mar his fortune. She on the other hand, was not in want of a decent support, and her principles forbad her acceptance of his offer. Grief for such ill treatment threw her into a consumption, and she died in a few months after.

When it was too late, the young gentleman repented, and was almost raving with the consciousness of having acted so basely. He desired to see me, and said " O my friend, how shall I banish from my heart, the remembrance of my dear *Caroline!*—How shall I forget the last parting scene.—It is but to die, she said—though it be a death of torture!—With my last breath will I pray for your prosperity! It is the decree of heaven that I should be thus chastised—thy will, O God, be done! May the remembrance of my sad fate never disturb your breast, unless it should bleed with sympathetic sorrow for my guilt, and prepare your own soul for heaven!"

Reflections on what had passed, harrowed up his soul. His reason was soon afterwards impaired. He

He was often seen walking by himself, and bursting into an agony, crying out, '*O Caroline! Caroline! I was thy murderer.*' He was indeed the wicked occasion of her death. He seldom slept above two hours at a time; and as certain as he awoke, the same thought occurred to his mind. His eyes looked hollow, his lips wore a livid paleness, as if he withered at the heart. His friends carried him into scenes of amusement, these made him sigh the more. He died soon after with melancholy.

Attend, my child, and take warning! I am assured of thy present innocency: I know thy mind agonizes whilst I am talking thus: but anxious as I am for thy safety, thou wilt forgive me, if I say too much. We are about to part, and it is fit I should communicate to thee, my knowledge of the ways of the world, and the means of shunning the evils of it.

O my child, I now declare to thee, in the awful presence of the God whom I adore, I had rather see thy blood stream from thy bosom, than behold thee in the arms, even of a king, on any terms but an honourable marriage, such as divine and human laws appoint for the virtuous. If thou wert to stray from virtue's sacred paths, though floods of briny tears would fall from thy fond father's eyes, these could not wash thee clean; but the day would come when they might rise in judgment against thee! Be on thy guard, and provoke not the wrath of Heaven!

DISCOURSE XXIX.

Advantages of the married state, when carefully engaged in. Fable of the two hounds. Dangerous effects of jealousy. Story of Harry Winton. Story of Jane Sprightly. The great duty of tenderness for children.

THIS is the last day in which I may enjoy a fair opportunity of communicating my thoughts to thee with such freedom, as divine providence has hitherto indulged us with. Since the time thou wert capable of listening to the voice of reason, and of forming thy mind to a relish of truth, I have not felt a greater satisfaction.

The subject of our conversation yesterday, naturally leads us to the consideration of *marriage*. The many mischiefs with which the lawless commerce of the sexes abounds, turn in favour of this honourable alliance.

Marriage ought to be in high estimation among men, not only as the state most safe to virtue, and in which so great a part of private happiness consists; but as best calculated to promote the welfare of our country. The Almighty, in the great order of his providence, having made the sexes for the mutual aid and support of each other; it is highly reasonable to presume, that when people come to an age of judgment, and are wealthy, or fit to get their bread by their skill or labour, marriage is the proper state of life; and nothing can be a stronger incentive to it, than the affections implanted in the human breast, which seek their object.

Happy it is when this union is cemented by a suitableness of disposition. Piety is the only bond that never fails; but I have seen the sad effects arising from such perverseness of humour, that even *common prudence* could not influence or restrain persons so connected, to be obliging and condescending to each other.

The extreme folly of a contrary conduct, is illustrated by the fable of the *two hounds*. They are represented as very fond of each other, but being young dogs, the huntsman coupled them, to prevent their following every scent, and hunting disorderly: they expressed great uneasiness at their situation; if one chose to go this way, the other was eager to go the contrary, till at length they came to a downright quarrel. An old hound, who had observed what was passing, reproved them in these terms: " What a couple of silly puppies you are, to be perpetually worrying yourselves at this rate! What hinders your going on peaceably and quietly together? Cannot you compromise the matter, by consulting each others inclination? Try to make a virtue of necessity, and submit to what you cannot remedy. You cannot get rid of the chain, but you may make it sit easy; and you will find by expe-

experience that mutual compliances, not only compensate for restraint, but are attended with delight."

I have heard it seriously maintained, that the misery of servants may be dated from their marriage day. Such an uncomfortable doctrine supposes that their wages are no ways equal to the expence when they have any children to provide for. This opinion proves too much; experience may be appealed to against it, as well as for it. Those who are extravagant or indolent, are hardly fit to be trusted in the marriage state; and the child born to such parents, comes into the world under a great disadvantage: But marriage sometimes awakens the attention of the most thoughtless, and every one may observe, that the industrious and provident, and such as are virtuously inclined, generally succeed in wedlock.

As to the proper time of marriage; if thou shouldst have a prudent offer, and there is no weighty reason to the contrary, accept it: marry in the early part of life: but if thy youth, and thy middle age pass without marriage, continue single. Whether thou marriest a young man, or one of middle age, consult his temper, and carefully avoid giving him offence; above all, I warn thee against *jealousy*. Teach not thy husband, if a young man, an evil lesson against thyself; nor make the elder thy distressed friend, or secret enemy. As there can be no government where there is no ruler, she who hath more sense than her husband, will shew it by her prudence and fear of God; still yielding the superiority to him, whom God hath set over her: she may perchance secretly influence his conduct; but openly to assume the *command*, except in very extraordinary cases, is a proof that her understanding falls very short of the true mark.

Rather think how to forgive real offences in thy husband, than create imaginary ones. If once the mind is possessed with a jealous frenzy, it loses the exercise of reason; and every object that relates to love, is armed with the stings of scorpions, to poison peace.

Give *jealousy* to the wind, and banish *disquiet*. Wert thou persuaded of real infidelity in thy husband, yet if thou hast a wish to share his heart, regain his affection, and turn it into its proper channel; be assured that if he hath any sensibility, thy tenderness and love, with his recollection of what religion requires, will subdue his false desires, and by the stings of conscience *convert* him. If he hath no sentiment of virtue, rage and resentment on thy part, will only aggravate thy misfortune, and make two great evils instead of one.

As to the *revenge* which some women take, it is not so much a proof of resentment, as of an evil inclination: it is a symptom of a sick and crazed mind: it is like a man's murdering himself because another has attempted to kill him: for she who proceeds to the extremity of repaying such an injury by prostitution, does but plunge a dagger into her own bosom; as if she were the aggressor, and meant to seek her punishment, even in the destruction of *her own soul.*

Command thyself, my child: patience and good humour almost work miracles; and I hope these will always secure thy husband's love, that thy days may pass in an uninterrupted tranquillity; in all fortunes remembering, that religion is then of most use, when the greatest calamity invades us; and that a calm resignation to the will of heaven, is the grand medicine which cures all the evils incident to human life.

If a woman discovers, that meekness, modesty, and prudence in living according to the circumstances of her husband, are her truest ornaments, she will likewise find wherein her interest consists. The proverb says, " The foot on the cradle, and the hand on the distaff, is the sign of a good housewife." This teaches that a woman inclined to virtue and industry, is at once able to manage her family, retain the affection of her husband, and educate her children according to her condition. Nothing can be so desirable to a man as such a wife!

Happy had it been for *Harry Winter*, if he had preferred *Sally Sweet*, to *Rebecca Wander!* He acknowledged *Sally*'s perfections; but in his eyes, the air, the grace, the form of *Rebecca*, were irresistible, and at length he married her. She had been used to the triumphs of beauty, and never rightly informed of any thing *substantially good*. She is of so impetuous a temper, as not to brook contradiction. Her resentments are as keen, as her vanity is uncontrolable. All her husband's wages are hardly sufficient to find her in ribbands. Where is their mighty love!—They are parting with mutual disgust. Poor *Harry* is much to be pitied. " Though a virtuous woman is a crown to her husband, she that maketh ashamed, is rottenness in his bones!"

In common cases of marriage, neither party being very wicked, it is with husband and wife, as with master and servant; if on one side the parties faithfully perform their duty, they can scarcely be extremely miserable. *Jane Sprightly* is young and lively, and much beloved by her husband; she desired him the other day to carry her to the fair, which he declined, giving her many reasons for so doing; adding " my dear *Jane*, you look as if you
" were displeased! What are all the *fairs* in the
" world to me, or all the women that attend them,
" compared to your smiles? I can bear any thing
" rather than your frowns, except the consciousness
" of doing that, which in its effects would hurt you:
" I would not do you harm for the world; not even
" at your own request; and no one can judge so
" well as myself, what will hurt you." *Jane* has good sense and candour, and heard him attentively. He spoke with such persuasive eloquence in regard to the sincerity of his love, she could no longer resist; but smoothing her brow, with a sweet smiling air, she said, " In good faith, my dear *Joshua*,
" though I had a fancy for the *fair*, it was but a
" fancy, and I believe thou art in the right: give
" me

"me thy hand, as a token of calm obedience and sincere affection; and she kissed it eagerly." Thus a proper exertion of prudence on one side, may in the issue be of essential importance to both.

To this end I will give thee another lesson, founded on the plainest sense and reason. The ready way to secure thy husband's affection and duty, is to be truly affectionate and dutiful as a wife; and always as agreeable as thou canst.

Whether thou should'st marry or remain single, cherish in thy bosom a tenderness for children: The woman devoid of this affection, hardly deserves the *name of a woman*. This affection relates to the community. Children are a large part of mankind; and childhood being without guile, it is at once an object of our love and respect. Remember the regard which was shewn to children by the Saviour of the world, when in allusion to their innocency, he declared, " of such are the kingdom of heaven:" My master used to say, that no compliment ever pleased him more, than that imputed to one of our great poets; that he was a *man in sense*, but in the simplicity of his manners, *a child*.

DISCOURSE XXX.

Conclusion of advice recommending filial piety, obedience to parents, and fidelity in service.

BE of good cheer, my child! If it should please the Almighty to bless thee with a husband, a good man, who may understand the value of thy virtues, thou mayest mend thy condition, by parting with me: but learn how to value the good which providence presents thee, be it what it may, and submit to the dispensations of heaven. If thou should'st marry and have *children*, thou wilt be the better subject, and mayest be more distinguished among thy equals or superiors. But teach thy children the fear of God, lest they prove a curse.

There is but a small portion of happiness which falls to the lot of individuals; none without some mixture, in the cup of life. But whilst thou entertainest thyself with hopes of bettering thy condition by marriage, forget not *me*, forget not " that whoso " honoureth his father shall have joy of his own " children, and when he maketh his prayer he shall " be heard;" as if the Almighty would not hear the prayers of those who neglect or despise their parents. These are high promises of exalted happiness. The wise man goes on: " Honour thy " father with thy whole heart, and forget not *the*

" *for-*

"*sorrows* of thy mother." This conveys a charming idea of maternal tenderness: and the love of thy dear mother, deserves indeed to be revered, even to her ashes! He then reminds us of the curse which attends the undutiful: " The eye that mocketh his father, and despiseth to obey his mother, the ravens of the valley shall pick it out, and the young eagles shall eat it." Is not this a beautiful allusion to that blindness and perverseness which leads some to neglect, and some even to insult their parents: it denounces the judgement they may expect, either by some temporal calamity, or by the vengeance of heaven which will overtake them. Such offences are of the blackest dye.

" Our parents, can never be requited:" Such is the nature of our obligations to them! Do not forsake me, my child, if I should need thy help: God only can tell what may happen! It is not the custom of our days, for children to be so attentive to their aged parents, as is required by the laws of God, and the obligations of society. In our condition, I fear some old people are thrown on the parochial charity, whose children might provide for them.

There are many countries where the inhabitants are short of us, in some respects, yet excel in the duty of children to parents. I remember to have heard my master say, that the *Gallicians*, who are labourers in the great cities of Portugal; and the *Russians*, who do the same offices in their own country,

country, are never so happy as when they carry home their gains, to assist their aged parents.

Children ought to honour their parents at all times, that their children may help them; and that the *great Father of mankind* may be their friend, and their days long in the land, wherein God hath given them life and health, to enjoy these blessings, in the stations which his providence hath appointed them.

Next to these are masters and mistresses. If thou should'st live many years in one place, married or single, I charge thee to remember that old servants are apt to presume upon their long service; it is but just that they should be esteemed for their probity, but not for impertinency. I have heard it said, " My master will not part with me, because I have " lived so long with him." This is not good reasoning: It should be rather said, " My master has " a good opinion of my fidelity, therefore I will " continue faithful, and retain my humility and " attention to his commands, or he will grow sick " of me. If I attempt to dictate to him, or make a " defence, when I should hold my tongue, or pro-" mise more care for the future, he will be a fool " if he keeps me; but if I should think him a fool I " should not therefore treat him insolently."

If a mutual regard, founded on a mutual service, be not supported on sound principles, whether in long or short service, married or single life, domestic service becomes unpleasant, and often borders upon that discontent, which is irreligious.

Beware

Beware of depending on my purse. Heaven knows I have little to give thee but my good advice. Do not however think this a misfortune; for the riches of the wealthy often prove temptations to great wickedness. I have known young persons so impatient to possess the goods of their parents, as to think they lived too long! Was not this horrible? It is to be hoped that we, who are poor, are in less danger of such rank iniquity.

Whatever sufferings thou mayest undergo, be courageous: remember that thy great Lord and Master *lived in poverty, and died in pain.* Never forget his life and death! To give thy mind true and just impressions of christianity, has been the main scope of my design: this hath been the bent of all the care and instruction which I have bestowed on thee; and whatever the *great* may apprehend to the contrary, I think this of such consequence, that no education can be called good, where it is wanting.

To-morrow we must part, but I trust that in love of God and goodness, we shall never be disunited! My solemn request is, that as often as the day begins and ends, thou wilt not barely *say thy prayers,* but *pray.* Strive to offer up thy heart in the pure flame of thy devotion, that when all thy days are brought to an end, thou mayest be prepared for eternity! Be not cast down but comforted: " The sorrow of the world," says the great Apostle, " worketh death, but, a godly sorrow worketh

L " repent-

" repentance to falvation." Let a fenfe of *virtue* be thy conftant *joy!*

There needs no further meffenger from heaven, to tell us that we are *all finful*, and except we repent we muft *all perifh*; but we fee how merciful *our heavenly Father is*, if we do repent. Learn of St. Paul, to reafon like a rational and accountable being, " if God fpared not *his own Son*, but delivered him " up for us *all*, how will he not, with him alfo, " freely give us *all things?*" Is not this an argument that the weakeft may underftand, and which the wifeft muft admire! May the righteous God uphold thee in thy paths! Let them be fuch as are pleafing to him, as far as thou canft difcover, and whether in life or death, all will be well! My dear child, farewel!

CONCLUSION XXXI.

Prayer for repentance and reconciliation adapted to the ftate of human nature, and fuch as believe in Chrift.

HEAR me, O Lord of life! ponder my meditations, and confider the longings of my foul to ferve and worfhip thee! When I look back on thy wonders of old, and the mercies which thou haft fhewn to all the children of men: when I contemplate the prefervation I have experienced in my own perfon, in ficknefs and danger, my heart is

exalted

exalted with joy, and my spirit resteth in the hope of the continuance of thy goodness to me, even for ever and ever!

Yet am I unworthy to stand in thy sight, O God, for my transgressions and infirmities are numberless! Give me thy aid to sue for thy pardon! Vouchsafe to grant me such a measure of patience and humility, meekness and temperance, fortitude and benevolence, that my thoughts being subdued by righteousness, my words and actions may be acceptable in thy sight. Purify my imagination, and banish the foolishness of my thoughts, which so often interrupts the repose of my mind! I am sinful in habit, imperfect in nature, and not worthy to look up to heaven! yet, O God, thou knowest whereof I am made: make me so watchful and resolute, that I may never fall again from thee.

Thy judgments, O Lord, are right; and in faithfulness hast thou caused me to be troubled. The soul that is troubled, and the spirit that is vexed, crieth unto thee! Hear me, O God, my Father, and turn thee unto me according to the multitude of thy mercies!—Let the remembrance of my past misdeeds be blotted out, and cleanse me from my secret faults: let not the sins, to which I am by temper and constitution prone, prevail against me.

O Father Almighty, grant me such a measure of thy grace, that I may daily learn *how to repent*; and so apply myself to the discharge of my duty, that when my feet shall slip, thou in thy goodness mayest uphold me!

Give me a contrite heart, O God, that I may worthily lament my sins: and make such confession of them, as thou shalt please to accept! Comfort me, O Lord, that I may not be cast down: and let thy reconciliation, through the intercession of my blessed Lord, restore my heart to joy!

O remember not my sins past, and the errors of my ways, but look on me a miserable sinner, with eyes of compassion, for I am come to great misery. Feed me with the bread of tears, and give me plenteousness of tears to drink, but shew me the light of thy countenance, and my soul will be restored to health.—According to the greatness of thy power, preserve me in the hour of death and in the day of judgment!

Inspire my heart with christian charity for all my fellow-creatures; and let the sorrowful sighing of the prisoner come before thee. Relieve the contrite heart according to thy wonted favour, and them who are suffering in poverty, or pain, or mourning under any affliction.

Conduct me, O Lord, as a sheep of thy pasture, that my soul may rejoice in giving thee thanks, and in every passage of my life shew forth thy praise!

Let thy spirit lead me forth, and direct my paths in righteousness: that with zeal and truth, purity and singleness of heart, I may discharge thy will on earth, as far as my imperfect nature will admit, as it is done in heaven!

Grant that I may keep in constant view, the life and death of the blessed Saviour of the world, that through faith in his promises, I may obtain remission of my sins. Let me consecrate every hour of my life to his example; that all the glories of this transient scene may appear as darkness and horror, in comparison of the wisdom which springeth from hope in that immortal life which he hath promised!

Give me thy grace, O Lord, so to arrest my fleeting hours, that I may compass all the pious and rational designs at which my soul aspires. Let me act as a chosen instrument of thy mercies to mankind: that in every condition, the happiness of others may be the constant subject of my joy!

Banish from me all anxious desires, that I may possess my spirit in freedom and resignation; and suffer neither the noise and bustle of the world, nor the deluding blandishments of sense, to captivate my heart; but whilst my body tends to its original dust, whether in health, or labouring in pain, the strength of my mind may grow to maturity; and my soul rejoice in the contemplation of the happiness of the just, in the blissful regions of immortality!

Cherish and strengthen my hopes, that whatever thy wisdom shall ordain, concerning the time which thou shalt yet permit me to live on earth, I may resolutely pursue that which is right in thy sight; and whilst I enter into the recesses of my own mind, and compassionate the faults of others, let me unbosom my thoughts to thee, in whose friendship there can be no disappointment!

Give me a true understanding of the honour and love, which I owe to my king, my country, and all
the

the human race: but let no flattery, distinction, or false bias, sully the purity of my love and gratitude towards thee, O God! or divert the current of my thoughts from the fountain of reason, and the source of felicity!

Let the ends of the earth *remember thee*, and all nations fall down before thee!——Cherubims and Seraphims, and all the numerous host of heaven, pay homage unutterable by mortal tongue, before the majesty of thy throne! O Father omnipotent, reject not my humble praise!

Thou, thou art *all!*—To thee, O God, I offer up my prayer, in the hour I rise from the death of sleep, 'till my senses are locked again in darkness. Let all my hopes, and all my wishes center in thee, and be directed to thy glory!

Fill my heart with such knowledge of thy wisdom, thy goodness, and thy justice, that delighting in thy laws, I may dwell under the shadow of thy mercy! Let my remembrance of thee be sweeter than the praises of an applauding world; as the riches of thy wisdom exceed all earthly treasure! Whether my life shall find honour or disgrace, evil or good report, suffer not my mind to be enslaved by dissipation; nor any custom or delusion of the world, divert my heart from thy truth!

Strengthen my faith in thee, O God, from day to day! And let my knowledge of thy sacred word, transmitted down from age to age, guide and direct my steps; that *reason* being enlightened by thy *grace*, my *faith* may grow to maturity, and seeing and ap-

proving

proving what is juſt and holy, I may adore thy unchangeable perfections!

Thou, O mighty Lord of heaven, who covereſt the earth as with a cloud; and extendeſt the rays of thy omniſcience over all Beings:——Thou whoſe wiſdom is profounder than the deep, and brighter than the meridian ſun, infinite in all perfection!—make thy will appear to me, clear as the light, and bright as the glories of the day; that diſcerning thy laws, I may inflexibly abide in thy ſtatutes.

Shed thy influence on my ſoul, O Lord Almighty! that ſhunning all practices which *weaken faith and diſturb reaſon*, I may poſſeſs ſuch fortitude as will always keep me ſteady in thy paths. Thou art *Truth*; and all my reſearches in which I remember thee not, are full of error and deluſion!

Strengthen the powers of my mind, O God, that I may collect my ſcattered thoughts and exerciſe them in that which is agreeable to thee, till the approaching time arrives, when by thy mercy, I may behold with my eyes, the brightneſs of thy incomprehenſible wiſdom and glory!

Teach me to meet my diſſolution with an humble, contrite, and undaunted heart; and O my father, my friend, my God! let me die the death of the righteous; that when I ſhall appear at the tribunal of *Chriſt*, I may hear his ſentence in extaſy of joy, and become a ſubject of the kingdom of Heaven!

O Merciful, Omniſcient, Omnipotent Father of angels, and men, accept my humble prayer!—From my inmost soul, I beseech thee to hear me! Stretch forth thy mighty arm to deliver me from my numberless offences, and all the anxious and turbulent discords of men, that I may resign my breath in peace!—And bring me, O merciful Father, to thine everlasting joy, for the sake of Jesus Christ my Redeemer, who died on the cross for the sins of the world! AMEN.

THE END.

www.ingramcontent.com/pod-product-compliance
Lightning Source LLC
Chambersburg PA
CBHW021841230426
43669CB00008B/1044